AAT

Level 3

Diploma in Accounting

Management Accounting Techniques

Question Bank

For assessments from
September 2022

First edition 2021

ISBN 9781 5097 4369 8
eISBN 9781 5097 4277 6

British Library Cataloguing-in-Publication Data
A catalogue record for this book is available
from the British Library

Published by

BPP Learning Media Ltd
BPP House, Aldine Place
142-144 Uxbridge Road
London W12 8AA

www.bpp.com/learningmedia

Printed in the United Kingdom

Your learning materials, published by BPP
Learning Media Ltd, are printed on paper
obtained from traceable sustainable sources.

All rights reserved. No part of this publication
may be reproduced, stored in a retrieval system
or transmitted in any form or by any means,
electronic, mechanical, photocopying, recording
or otherwise, without the prior written
permission of BPP Learning Media.

The contents of this course material are
intended as a guide and not professional advice.
Although every effort has been made to ensure
that the contents of this course material are
correct at the time of going to press, BPP
Learning Media makes no warranty that the
information in this course material is accurate or
complete and accept no liability for any loss or
damage suffered by any person acting or
refraining from acting as a result of the material
in this course material.

We are grateful to the AAT for permission to
reproduce the sample assessment(s). The
answers to the sample assessment(s) have been
published by the AAT. All other answers have
been prepared by BPP Learning Media Ltd.

©
BPP Learning Media Ltd
2021

A note about copyright

Dear Customer

What does the little © mean and why
does it matter?

Your market-leading BPP books, course
materials and e-learning materials do not
write and update themselves. People write
them on their own behalf or as employees
of an organisation that invests in this
activity. Copyright law protects their
livelihoods. It does so by creating rights
over the use of the content.

Breach of copyright is a form of theft – as
well as being a criminal offence in some
jurisdictions, it is potentially a serious
breach of professional ethics.

With current technology, things might
seem a bit hazy but, basically, without
the express permission of BPP Learning
Media:

- Photocopying our materials is a
  breach of copyright

- Scanning, ripcasting or conversion of
  our digital materials into different file
  formats, uploading them to Facebook
  or e-mailing them to your friends is a
  breach of copyright

You can, of course, sell your books, in the
form in which you have bought them –
once you have finished with them. (Is this
fair to your fellow students? We update
for a reason.) Please note the e-products
are sold on a single user licence basis: we
do not supply 'unlock' codes to people
who have bought them secondhand.

And what about outside the UK? BPP
Learning Media strives to make our
materials available at prices students can
afford by local printing arrangements,
pricing policies and partnerships which
are clearly listed on our website. A tiny
minority ignore this and indulge in
criminal activity by illegally photocopying
our material or supporting organisations
that do. If they act illegally and
unethically in one area, can you really
trust them?

Contents

Question and Answer bank

Introduction

This is BPP Learning Media's AAT Question Bank for *Management Accounting Techniques*. It is part of a suite of ground-breaking resources produced by BPP Learning Media for AAT assessments.

This Question Bank has been written in conjunction with the BPP Course Book, and has been carefully designed to enable students to practise all of the learning outcomes and assessment criteria for the units that make up *Management Accounting Techniques*. It is fully up to date as at November 2021 and reflects both the AAT's qualification specification and the sample assessments provided by the AAT.

This Question Bank contains these key features:

*   Tasks corresponding to each chapter of the Course Book. Some tasks are designed for learning purposes, others are of assessment standard

The emphasis in all tasks and assessments is on the practical application of the skills acquired.

VAT

You may find tasks throughout this Question Bank that need you to calculate or be aware of a rate of VAT. This is stated at 20% in these examples and questions.

Approaching the assessment

When you sit the assessment it is very important that you follow the on screen instructions. This means you need to carefully read the instructions, both on the introduction screens and during specific tasks.

When you access the assessment you should be presented with an introductory screen with information similar to that shown below (taken from the introductory screen from one of the AAT's AQ2022 sample assessments for *Management Accounting Techniques*).

Assessment information

You have **2 hours and 30 minutes** to complete this practice assessment.

- This assessment contains **6 tasks** and you should attempt to complete **every task,**
- Each task is independent. You will not need to refer to your answers to previous tasks.
- The total number of marks for this assessment is **120.**
- Read every task carefully to make sure you understand what is required.
- Where the date is relevant, it is given in the task data.
- Both minus signs and brackets can be used to indicate negative numbers **unless** task instructions state otherwise.
- You must use a full stop to indicate a decimal point. For example, write 100.57 **not** 100,57 or 10057.
- You may use a comma to indicate a number in the thousands, but you don't have to. For example, 10000 and 10,000 are both acceptable.

The actual instructions will vary depending on the subject you are studying for. It is very important you read the instructions on the introductory screen and apply them in the assessment. You don't want to lose marks when you know the correct answer just because you have not entered it in the right format.

In general, the rules set out in the AAT sample assessments for the subject you are studying for will apply in the real assessment, but you should carefully read the information on this screen again in the real assessment, just to make sure. This screen may also confirm the VAT rate used if applicable.

A full stop is needed to indicate a decimal point. We would recommend using minus signs to indicate negative numbers and leaving out the comma signs to indicate thousands, as this results in a lower number of key strokes and less margin for error when working under time pressure. Having said that, you can use whatever is easiest for you as long as you operate within the rules set out for your particular assessment.

You have to show competence throughout the assessment and you should therefore complete all of the tasks. Don't leave questions unanswered.

In some assessments, written or complex tasks may be human marked. In this case you are given a blank space or table to enter your answer into. You are told in the assessments which tasks these are (note: there may be none if all answers are marked by the computer).

If these involve calculations, it is a good idea to decide in advance how you are going to lay out your answers to such tasks by practising answering them on a word document, and certainly you should try all such tasks in this Question Bank and in the AAT's environment using the sample assessment.

When asked to fill in tables, or gaps, never leave any blank even if you are unsure of the answer. Fill in your best estimate.

Note that for some assessments where there is a lot of scenario information or tables of data provided (eg tax tables), you may need to access these via 'pop-ups'. Instructions will be provided on how you can bring up the necessary data during the assessment.

Finally, take note of any task specific instructions once you are in the assessment. For example you may be asked to enter a date in a certain format or to enter a number to a certain number of decimal places.

Grading

To achieve the qualification and to be awarded a grade, you must pass all the mandatory unit assessments, all optional unit assessments (where applicable) and the synoptic assessment.

The AAT Level 3 Diploma in Accounting will be awarded a grade. This grade will be based on performance across the qualification. Unit assessments are not individually graded. These assessments are given a mark that is used in calculating the overall grade.

How overall grade is determined

You will be awarded an overall qualification grade (Distinction, Merit, and Pass). If you do not achieve the qualification you will not receive a qualification certificate, and the grade will be shown as unclassified.

The marks of each assessment will be converted into a percentage mark and rounded up or down to the nearest whole number. This percentage mark is then weighted according to the weighting of the unit assessment or synoptic assessment within the qualification. The resulting weighted assessment percentages are combined to arrive at a percentage mark for the whole qualification.

Grade definition	Percentage threshold
Distinction	90–100%
Merit	80–89%
Pass	70–79%
Unclassified	0–69% Or failure to pass one or more assessment/s

Re-sits

Some AAT qualifications such as the AAT Advanced Diploma in Accounting have restrictions in place for how many times you are able to re-sit assessments. Please refer to the AAT website for further details.

You should only be entered for an assessment when you are well prepared and you expect to pass the assessment.

AAT qualifications

The material in this book may support the following AAT qualifications:

AAT Level 3 Diploma in Accounting
AAT Diploma in Accounting at SCQF Level 7

Supplements

From time to time we may need to publish supplementary materials to one of our titles. This can be for a variety of reasons. From a small change in the AAT unit guidance to new legislation coming into effect between editions.

You should check our supplements page regularly for anything that may affect your learning materials. All supplements are available free of charge on our supplements page on our website at:

www.bpp.com/learning-media/about/students

Improving material and removing errors

There is a constant need to update and enhance our study materials in line with both regulatory changes and new insights into the assessments.

From our team of authors BPP appoints a subject expert to update and improve these materials for each new edition.

Their updated draft is subsequently technically checked by another author and from time to time, non-technically checked by a proof reader.

We are very keen to remove as many numerical errors and narrative typos as we can but given the volume of detailed information being changed in a short space of time we know that a few errors will sometimes get through our net.

We apologise in advance for any inconvenience that an error might cause. We continue to look for new ways to improve these study materials and would welcome your suggestions. If you have any comments about this book, please email nisarahmed@bpp.com or write to Nisar Ahmed, AAT Head of Programme, BPP Learning Media Ltd, BPP House, Aldine Place, London W12 8AA.

Question Bank

BPP
LEARNING
MEDIA

Chapter 1 – Introduction to management accounting

Task 1.1

Drag and drop the correct answers into the table below:

Annual
External to the organisation
Historic
Historic and future
Internal management
Specified by law
To be useful
When required

	Financial accounting	Management accounting
Users		
Timing		
Type of information		
Format		

Task 1.2

Drag and drop the correct answers into the table below:

Materials
Non-production overheads
Prime cost
Production cost
Production overheads
Total cost

Cost card	£
Direct [ ]	X
Direct labour	X
Direct expenses	X
[ ]	X
[ ]	X
[ ]	X
[ ]	
– selling and distribution	X
– administration	X
– finance	X
[ ]	X

BPP
LEARNING
MEDIA

Task 1.3

What is the purpose of management information?

	✓
Planning only	
Planning and control only	
Planning, control and decision-making only	
Planning, control, decision-making and research and development	

Task 1.4

Prime cost is:

	✓
All costs incurred in manufacturing a product	
The total of direct costs	
The material cost of a product	
The cost of operating a department	

Task 1.5

You are an accounts assistant at J Co, a business which makes wooden toy soldiers. You have been asked to present a cost card for the toy soldiers using the following information.

Drag and drop the correct answers into the table below and insert the corresponding figures:

	£
Advertising and sales promotion	0.70
Hire of special tools	0.50
Rent, rates, light and heat	0.30
Toy makers' wages	3.00
Wood and paint	3.50

Cost card – toy soldier	£
Direct materials [ ]	
Direct labour [ ]	
Direct expenses [ ]	
Prime cost	
[ ]	
Production cost	
Non-production overheads:	
[ ]	
Total cost	

Task 1.6

Match the fundamental ethical principle to the correct description below by dragging the appropriate option into the table.

Description	Principle
Complying with relevant laws and regulations	
Not disclosing information to third parties without authority	
Being straightforward and honest in all professional and business relationships	
Not allowing bias or conflict of interest	
Maintaining professional knowledge and skill	

Professional competence and due care

Integrity

Confidentiality

Professional behaviour

Objectivity

Task 1.7

Segmented cost is:

	✓
All revenues relating to a particular product made by the business	
The total of direct costs relating to a particular product made by the business	
The material cost relating to a particular product made by the business	
The costs relating to a component of the business which generates revenue	

Task 1.8

Identify whether the following statements about budgets are true or false.

	True ✓	False ✓
A budget is used as part of an organisation's planning process		
A budget can be used for cost control		

BPP LEARNING MEDIA

Chapter 2 – Cost classification and cost behaviour

Task 2.1

Drag and drop the correct entries into the table below, based on whether each one would be classified as a production cost, a selling and distribution cost or an administration cost:

Depreciation of delivery vans
Depreciation of plant and machinery
Factory heat and light
Finance Director's salary
Fuel and oil for delivery vans
Sales Director's salary

Cost types	
Production cost	
Selling and distribution cost	
Administration cost	

Task 2.2

Which of the following would be classed as indirect labour?

	✓
A coach driver in a transport company	
Machine operators in a milk bottling plant	
A maintenance assistant in a factory maintenance department	
Plumbers in a construction company	

Task 2.3

Which of the following items would be treated as an indirect cost?

	✓
Wood used to make a chair	
Metal used for the legs of a chair	
Fabric to cover the seat of a chair	
Staples to fix the fabric to the seat of a chair	

Task 2.4

A company employs three drivers to deliver goods to its customers. The salaries paid to these drivers are:

	✓
A part of prime cost	
A direct production expense	
A production overhead	
A selling and distribution overhead	

Task 2.5

L Ltd is a badminton racquet manufacturer.

Drag and drop the correct entries into the box below to match the correct cost type to each cost item.

Administration costs
Direct labour
Direct materials
Indirect labour
Selling and distribution costs

Cost types	
Carbon for racquet heads	
Office stationery	
Wages of employees stringing racquets	
Supervisors' salaries	
Advertising stand at badminton tournaments	

Task 2.6

Look at the two graphs below. **What costs do they depict?**

Graph A

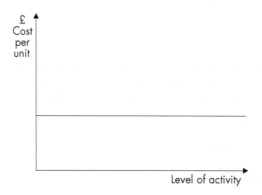

Graph B

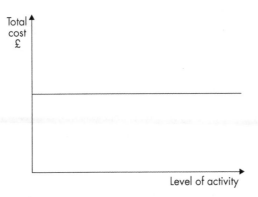

Total cost £

Level of activity

Graph A

	✓
Variable cost per unit	
Fixed cost per unit	
Total fixed cost across level of activity	
Total variable cost	

Graph B

	✓
Variable cost per unit	
Fixed cost per unit	
Total fixed cost across level of activity	
Total variable cost	

Task 2.7

Calculate the fixed and variable elements of the following costs using the high-low technique:

Month	Output Units	Total cost £
January	16,000	252,500
February	18,500	290,000
March	24,000	372,500
April	26,500	410,000
May	25,500	395,000

The following information relates to Tasks 2.8 to 2.12

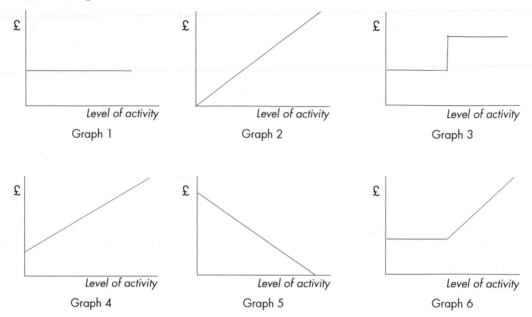

£	£	£
Level of activity	*Level of activity*	*Level of activity*
Graph 1	Graph 2	Graph 3
£	£	£
Level of activity	*Level of activity*	*Level of activity*
Graph 4	Graph 5	Graph 6

Which one of the above graphs illustrates the costs described in tasks 2.8 to 2.12?

Task 2.8

A variable cost – when the vertical axis represents cost incurred.

	✓
Graph 1	
Graph 2	
Graph 4	
Graph 5	

Task 2.9

A fixed cost – when the vertical axis represents cost incurred.

	✓
Graph 1	
Graph 2	
Graph 3	
Graph 6	

BPP
LEARNING
MEDIA

Task 2.10

A variable cost – when the vertical axis represents cost per unit.

	✓
Graph 1	
Graph 2	
Graph 3	
Graph 6	

Task 2.11

A semi-variable cost – when the vertical axis represents cost incurred.

	✓
Graph 1	
Graph 2	
Graph 4	
Graph 5	

Task 2.12

A step fixed cost – when the vertical axis represents cost incurred.

	✓
Graph 3	
Graph 4	
Graph 5	
Graph 6	

Task 2.13

A company has recorded the following data in the two most recent periods.

Total costs of production £	Volume of production Units
13,500	700
18,300	1,100

What is the best estimate of the company's fixed costs per period?

	✓
£13,500	
£13,200	
£5,100	
£4,800	

Task 2.14

We usually classify short-term costs into fixed, variable, step-fixed or semi-variable but in the long run, all costs are:

	✓
Fixed	
Variable	
Step-fixed	
Semi-variable	

Task 2.15

The following information is available for product Zed for the month of January.

Production costs:

Variable   £8 per unit
Fixed   £12,000

What is the total production cost of producing 8,000 units of product Zed in January?

£ [   ]

BPP
LEARNING
MEDIA

Chapter 3 – Materials and labour costs

Task 3.1

Paris Ltd manufactures a product the Lipsy, which requires plastic handles PH5:

- Annual demand 90,000 kilograms
- Annual holding cost per kilogram £1
- Fixed ordering cost £2

(a) Calculate the Economic Order Quantity (EOQ) for PH5.

The inventory record shown below for plastic grade PH5 for the month of September has only been fully completed for the first three weeks of the month.

(b) Complete the entries in the inventory record for the two receipts on 24 and 28 September that were ordered using the EOQ method (giving total cost to the nearest whole number).

(c) Complete ALL entries in the inventory record for the two issues in the month and for the closing balance at the end of September using the FIFO method of issuing inventory. (Show the costs per kilogram (kg) in £s to 3 decimal places; and the total costs in whole £s.)

Inventory record for plastic grade PH5:

| Date | Receipts | | | Issues | | | Balance | |
	Quantity kg	Cost per kg £	Total cost £	Quantity kg	Cost per kg £	Total cost £	Quantity kg	Total cost £
Balance as at 22 September							150	180
24 September		1.398						
26 September				400				
28 September		1.402						
30 September				500				

Task 3.2

Calculate the closing inventory value at 31 March using FIFO by completing the entries in the inventory record below. Enter the cost per unit to 1 decimal place and the total cost to the nearest whole pound.

Inventory record

Date	Receipts			Issues			Balance	
	Quantity kg	Cost per kg £	Total cost £	Quantity kg	Cost per kg £	Total cost £	Quantity kg	Total cost £
Balance as at 1 January							4,000	10,000
31 January	1,000		2,000					
15 February				3,000		7,500		
28 February	1,500		3,750					
14 March				500		1,250		

Task 3.3

Using the AVCO method calculate the cost of materials issues and the value of closing inventory using the information below.

Enter your answer onto the inventory record below. Important! Enter the cost per kg to 2 decimal places. Enter the total cost to the nearest whole pound.

1 January	Balance	300 kg	£25 per unit
2 January	Issue	250 kg	
12 January	Receipt	400 kg	£25.75 per unit
21 January	Issue	200 kg	
29 January	Issue	75 kg	

Inventory Record Card

Date	Purchases Quantity kg	Purchases Cost £	Purchases Total cost £	Requisitions Quantity kg	Requisitions Cost £	Requisitions Total cost £	Balance Quantity kg	Balance Total cost £
1 Jan								
2 Jan								
12 Jan								
21 Jan								
29 Jan								

Task 3.4

Fill in the table below using FIFO to calculate the closing valuation at 31 March.

Inventory record

Date	Receipts Quantity kg	Receipts Cost per kg £	Receipts Total cost £	Issues Quantity kg	Issues Cost per kg £	Issues Total cost £	Balance Quantity kg	Balance Total cost £
1 January	4,000	2.50	10,000				4,000	10,000
31 January	1,000		2,000					
15 February				3,000				
28 February	1,500	2.50					3,500	8,250
14 March				500				

BPP LEARNING MEDIA

Task 3.5

Sheap Ltd had the following containers of juice in inventory:

Date purchased	Quantity	Cost per container £	Total cost £
April 28	840	19.0	15,960
May 4	960	24.5	23,520
May 10	480	28.9	13,872

Drag and drop the correct cost into the cost column of the table to record issuing 850 of these containers on 11 May and to record the inventory balance after the issue using:

- AVCO (weighted average cost)
- FIFO (first in, first out)

	Cost £
AVCO issue	
FIFO issue	
AVCO balance	
FIFO balance	

£33,462	£37,147
£16,205	£19,890

Task 3.6

A company wishes to minimise its inventory costs. Order costs are £10 per order and holding costs are £0.10 per unit per month. Fall Co estimates **annual** demand to be 5,400 units.

The economic order quantity is [   ] units.

Task 3.7

The following data relates to component L512:

Ordering costs	£100 per order
Inventory holding costs	£8 per unit per annum
Annual demand	1,225 units

The economic order quantity is [   ] units (to the nearest whole unit).

BPP LEARNING MEDIA

Task 3.8

The following data relate to inventory item A452:

Average usage   100 units per day
Minimum usage   60 units per day
Maximum usage   130 units per day
Maximum inventory level   5,100
Lead time   20–26 days
Inventory buffer   1,080
EOQ   4,000 units

The reorder level is [   ] **units.**

The minimum inventory reorder quantity is [   ] **units.**

The maximum inventory reorder quantity is [   ] **units.**

Task 3.9

Production costs for June included direct materials of £40,000, direct labour of £30,000 and production overhead of £10,000. At the end of the month, 9,580 units were complete and 600 units were 70% complete.

Calculate the cost per equivalent unit. Enter your answer to the nearest whole number.

£ [   ]

Calculate the closing value of work in progress. Enter your answer to the nearest whole number.

£ [   ]

Task 3.10

A company operates an integrated accounting system.

The accounting entries for the issue to production of indirect materials from inventory would be:

Debit	Credit	✓
Production account	Inventory account	
Inventory account	Production overhead control account	
Production overhead control account	Inventory account	
Cost of sales account	Inventory account	

Task 3.11

Lol Ltd makes wooden bird boxes. Below are extracts from Lol Ltd's payroll for last week.

Date	Labour costs
8 June	Box manufacture: Production employees' pay 380 hours at £15 per hour
10 June	Box painting: Production employees' basic pay £2,100 + £250 overtime
12 June	Warehouse department Employees' pay £1,400 + 15% bonus
14 June	General Administration department: Staff salaries £3,400 + 20% bonus

Complete the cost journal entries to record the four payroll payments made last week.

Date	Code		Debit £	Credit £
8 June		▼		
8 June		▼		
10 June		▼		
10 June		▼		
12 June		▼		
12 June		▼		
14 June		▼		
14 June		▼		

Picklist:

OH01 Operating overheads
DI02 Box painting direct costs
OH02 Non-operating overheads
DI01 Box manufacture direct costs
WA01 Wages control account

Task 3.12

The ledger clerk has forgotten to complete the other entries needed for wages in the production account and the production overhead control account. **Input the correct entries in the two control accounts below.** Remember that £275,000 relates to direct labour and £75,000 to indirect labour.

Production account

		£			£
31 May	Wages control				

Production overhead control

		£			£
31 May	Wages control				

Task 3.13

Which one of the following groups of workers would be classified as indirect labour?

	✓
Machinists in an organisation manufacturing clothes	
Bricklayers in a house building company	
Maintenance workers in a shoe factory	

Task 3.14

In a typical cost ledger, the double entry for indirect labour cost incurred is:

		✓
DEBIT Wages control	CREDIT Overhead control	
DEBIT Admin overhead control	CREDIT Wages control	
DEBIT Overhead control	CREDIT Wages control	
DEBIT Wages control	CREDIT Admin overhead control	

Task 3.15

Extracts are given below from Gloworm Ltd's payroll for March.

Manufacturing department A production employees' wages	£18,500
Manufacturing department B production employees' wages	£22,500
Maintenance department employees' wages	£12,700
General admin department employees' salaries	£7,600

Complete the cost journal entries to record the payroll payments for March.

	Code	Dr £	Cr £
Manufacturing department A wages	▼		
Manufacturing department A wages	▼		
Manufacturing department B wages	▼		
Manufacturing department B wages	▼		
Maintenance department wages	▼		
Maintenance department wages	▼		
General admin department salaries	▼		
General admin department salaries	▼		

Picklist:

3400 Operating overheads
2400 Manufacturing department B direct costs
6000 Wages control account
3500 Non-operating overheads
2300 Manufacturing department A direct costs

Task 3.16

In a typical cost ledger, the double entry for direct wages cost incurred is:

		✓
DEBIT Wages control	CREDIT Production account	
DEBIT Production	CREDIT Wages control account	
DEBIT Costs of sales account	CREDIT Production account	
DEBIT Finished goods account	CREDIT Production account	

Task 3.17

Below is a table showing the hours worked by one of XYZ Ltd's employees, who is paid as follows:

- For a basic shift every day from Monday to Friday, the basic pay is £15 per hour.

- For any overtime in excess of the basic hours, on any day from Monday to Friday – the extra hours are paid at time-and-a-half (basic pay plus an overtime premium equal to half of basic pay).

- For any hours worked on Saturday or Sunday the hours are paid at double time (basic pay plus an overtime premium equal to basic pay).

(a) Complete the gaps in the table below to calculate the labour cost (to 2 decimal places).

Employee's weekly timesheet for week ending 7 December

	Hours	Total pay £
Basic pay (including basic hours for overtime)	48	
Mon–Fri overtime premium	7	
Sat–Sun overtime premium	6	
Total		

(b)   Employees are also entitled to a bonus of 30% of basic hourly rate for every unit of production in excess of the monthly target. The target for last month was 450 units and employee A produced 480 units.

What was employee A's bonus payment for the month?

£ [   ]

(c)   At the end of the month there was a total closing work in progress of 7,000 units which were 60% complete with regard to labour.

What are the equivalent units of production with regard to labour of the closing work in progress? [   ] units

Task 3.18

ABC Ltd produced 42,000 equivalent units of production in June. The total direct labour cost for June was £13,650.

Calculate the total direct labour cost per equivalent unit of the finished production for June.

Give your answer in £s to three decimal places.

£ [   ]

Task 3.19

Hopk Ltd has four employees working in department B. They are paid a basic rate of £22.00 per hour, and any overtime is paid at the following rates:

*   Overtime rate 1 – basic pay + 50%
*   Overtime rate 2 – double the rate of basic rate

Hopk sets a target for number of units produced each month. A bonus equal to 40% of the basic hourly rate is payable for each unit produced in the month in excess of the target.

The target for April for department B was 2,387.5 units; however, the team actually produced 2,987.5 units.

All team members work the same number of hours.

All overtime and bonuses are included as part of the direct labour cost.

(a)   Complete the gaps in the table below to calculate the total labour cost for department.

Labour cost	Hours	£
Basic pay	800	
Overtime rate 1	50	
Overtime rate 2	40	
Total cost before bonus	890	
Bonus payment		
Total cost including bonus		

(b)   Calculate the total labour cost of producing each unit in the month of April.

The total labour cost of producing each unit in the month of April is:

£ [   ] .

There are four employees in department B.

(c)   Complete the following sentence.

The basic pay and overtime for each member of department B for April was:

£ [   ] and the bonus payable to each team member was:

£ [   ] .

Chapter 4 – Allocation and apportionment

Task 4.1

Paris Ltd's budgeted overheads for the next financial year are:

	£	£
Depreciation of plant and equipment		2,010,375
Power for production machinery		1,787,500
Rent and rates		261,268
Light and heat		57,750
Indirect labour costs:		
Maintenance	253,750	
Stores	90,125	
General Administration	600,251	
Total indirect labour cost		944,126

The following information is also available:

Department	Net book value of plant and equipment	Production machinery power usage (KwH)	Floor space (square metres)	Number of employees
Production centres:				
Silicon moulding	3,600,000	1,145,000		15
Silicon extrusion	4,400,000	2,430,000		16
Support cost centres:				
Maintenance			8,000	4
Stores			10,000	5
General Administration			10,000	6
Total	8,000,000	3,575,000	28,000	46

Overheads are allocated or apportioned on the most appropriate basis. The total overheads of the support cost centres are then reapportioned to the two production centres using the direct method.

- 35% of the Maintenance cost centre's time is spent maintaining production machinery in the Silicon moulding production centre, and the remainder in the Silicon extrusion production centre.

- The Stores cost centre makes 40% of its issues to the Silicon moulding production centre, and 60% to the Silicon extrusion production centre.

 BPP LEARNING MEDIA

- General Administration supports the two production centres equally.

- There is no reciprocal servicing between the three support cost centres.

Complete the table showing the apportionment and reapportionment of overheads to the two production centres. Round to the nearest pound.

	Basis of apportionment	Silicon moulding £	Silicon extrusion £	Maintenance £	Stores £	General Admin £	Totals £
Depreciation of plant and equipment	NBV of Plant and equipment						
Power for production machinery	Production machinery power usage (KwH)						
Rent and rates	Floor space						
Light and heat	Floor space						
Indirect labour	Allocated						
Totals							
Reapportion Maintenance							
Reapportion Stores							
Reapportion General Admin							
Total overheads to production centres							

Task 4.2

(a) The financial controller at Paris Ltd is reviewing the basis of allocating the costs of the two production centres, and is considering using the number of employees instead of NBV and power usage. Recalculate the allocations and apportionments using headcount as a basis for these two cost centres. She has also decided that the silicon moulding cost centre uses far more general admin than the extrusion cost centre, and wants you to recalculate the apportionments using a ratio of 65:35. Use the dropdown screen to remind you of the data in the task.

Dropdown screen

Paris Ltd's budgeted overheads for the next financial year are:

	£	£
Depreciation of plant and equipment		2,010,375
Power for production machinery		1,787,500
Rent and rates		261,268
Light and heat		57,750
Indirect labour costs:		
Maintenance	253,750	
Stores	90,125	
General Administration	600,251	
Total indirect labour cost		944,126

The following information is also available:

Department	Net book value of plant and equipment	Production machinery power usage (KwH)	Floor space (square metres)	Number of employees
Production centres:				
Silicon moulding	3,600,000	1,145,000		15
Silicon extrusion	4,400,000	2,430,000		16
Support cost centres:				
Maintenance			8,000	4
Stores			10,000	5
General Administration			10,000	6
Total	8,000,000	3,575,000	28,000	46

Overheads are allocated or apportioned on the most appropriate basis. The total overheads of the support cost centres are then reapportioned to the two production centres using the direct method.

- 35% of the Maintenance cost centre's time is spent maintaining production machinery in the Silicon moulding production centre, and the remainder in the Silicon extrusion production centre.

- The Stores cost centre makes 40% of its issues to the Silicon moulding production centre, and 60% to the Silicon extrusion production centre.

BPP
LEARNING
MEDIA

- General Administration supports the two production centres, with 65% of its costs attributable to Silicon moulding and 35% attributable to Silicon extrusion.

- There is no reciprocal servicing between the three support cost centres.

Complete the table showing the apportionment and reapportionment of overheads to the two production centres.

	Basis of apportionment	Silicon moulding £	Silicon extrusion £	Maintenance £	Stores £	General Admin £	Totals £
Depreciation of plant and equipment	Headcount						
Power for production machinery	Headcount						
Rent and rates	Floor space						
Light and heat	Floor space						
Indirect labour	Allocated						
Totals							
Reapportion Maintenance							
Reapportion Stores							
Reapportion General Admin							
Total overheads to production centres							

(b) If you were the manager in charge of the silicon moulding cost centre would you be happy with the revised allocations?

_____

Task 4.3

Product Em has the following estimated costs per unit.

Product Em	£ per unit
Direct materials	5.50
Direct labour	7.20
Variable overheads	1.50
Fixed manufacturing overheads	2.30
Fixed administration, selling and distribution costs	1.70
Total costs	18.20

What is the full absorption cost of one unit of Em?

£

Task 4.4

Using the following data reapportion the overheads of Stores and Maintenance and General administration overheads to production departments X and Y using the direct method.

	Production		Service centres		
	X £	Y £	Stores £	Maintenance £	General administration overheads £
Allocated & Apportioned overheads	80,000	50,000	40,000	30,000	8,000
Value of machinery	8,000	7,000			

- 55% of the stores department's time is spent on production department X. The remaining time is spent on production department Y.

- The maintenance costs are to be apportioned between the production departments on the basis of value of machinery.

- General administration overheads are to be apportioned equally between the two production departments.

Direct method

	Production		Service centres		
	X £	Y £	Stores £	Maintenance £	General administration overheads £
Overheads					
Reapportion Stores					
Reapportion Maintenance					
Reapportion general admin overheads					
Total					

Task 4.5

Using the following data reapportion the overheads of Stores and Maintenance to production departments X and Y using the step-down method starting with Stores

	Production		Service centres	
	X £	Y £	Stores £	Canteen £
Allocated & Apportioned overheads	80,000	50,000	40,000	30,000
Number of employees	30	50	5	–

- 50% of the stores department's time is spent on production department X. 30% of stores department's time is spent on production department Y. 20% is spent on maintenance.

- The canteen costs are to be apportioned between the production departments on the basis of number of employees.

Step-down method

	Production		Service centres	
	X £	Y £	Stores £	Maintenance £
Allocated overhead				
Apportion stores				
Apportion maintenance				
Total				

BPP LEARNING MEDIA

Chapter 5 – Absorption costing

Task 5.1

(a) You have been asked to calculate the actual overhead absorbed based on £20 per hour for labour hours and £55 per hour for machine hours, and the following actual hours for labour and machinery:

	Silicon moulding	Silicon extrusion
Actual direct labour hours	21,222	17,144
Actual machine hours	8,459	6,501
Overhead absorbed – labour hrs		
Overhead absorbed – machine hrs		

(b) The actual overheads were found to be £425,799 for silicon moulding and £354,416 for silicon extrusion. Calculate any differences between the actual overheads at the end of the quarter and the overheads absorbed that you have just calculated.

	Silicon moulding	Silicon extrusion
Actual overheads (£)		
Difference – labour hours		
Difference – machine hours		

Task 5.2

Over-absorbed overheads always occur when:

	✓
Absorbed overheads exceed actual overheads	
Absorbed overheads exceed budgeted overheads	
Actual overheads exceed budgeted overheads	

The following information relates to Tasks 5.3 and 5.4

A company has the following actual and budgeted data for year 4.

	Budget	Actual
Labour hours	8,000 hrs	9,000 hrs
Variable production overhead per unit	£3	£3
Fixed production overheads	£360,000	£432,000
Sales	6,000 units	8,000 units

Overheads are absorbed using a rate per unit, based on budgeted labour hours.

Task 5.3

The fixed production overhead absorbed during year 4 was:

	✓
£384,000	
£405,000	
£432,000	
£459,000	

Task 5.4

Fixed production overhead was:

	✓
Under absorbed by £27,000	
Under absorbed by £72,000	
Under absorbed by £75,000	
Over absorbed by £27,000	

Task 5.5

Choose the correct description for each of the three terms below.

Term	Description	
Activity based costing		▼
Cost driver		▼
Cost pool		▼

Picklist:

Assigning only variable costs to cost units
A factor influencing the level of cost
Equivalent to a cost centre in traditional absorption costing
A cost which cannot be traced directly to a product
A unit of product for which costs can be ascertained
Charging whole cost items direct to a cost unit
Identifying activities which cause costs to charge overheads to products

Task 5.6

Paris Ltd has set its budgets and estimated its budgeted overheads and activity levels as follows:

	Silicon moulding	Silicon extrusion
Budgeted overheads (£)	450,000	352,520
Budgeted direct labour hours	25,350	20,475
Budgeted machine hours	8,750	6,350

(a) What would be the budgeted overhead absorption rate for each department, if this were set based on their both being heavily automated?

	✓
Silicon moulding £18/hour, Silicon extrusion £17/hour	
Silicon moulding £51/hour, Silicon extrusion £17/hour	
Silicon moulding £51/hour, Silicon extrusion £56/hour	
Silicon moulding £18/hour, Silicon extrusion £56/hour	

(b) What would be the budgeted overhead absorption rate for each department, if this were set based on their both being labour intensive?

	✓
Silicon moulding £51/hour, Silicon extrusion £17/hour	
Silicon moulding £18/hour, Silicon extrusion £17/hour	
Silicon moulding £18/hour, Silicon extrusion £56/hour	
Silicon moulding £51/hour, Silicon extrusion £56/hour	

Task 5.7

The financial controller at Paris Ltd has looked at the overhead absorption rates in the two cost centres, and wants a single rate for labour hours and for machinery across the two centres. She has chosen £20/hr for labour hours and £55/hr for machinery.

Recalculate the budgeted direct labour hours and machine hours based on these rates. Give your answers to the nearest whole number. Refer to the table below from the last task:

	Silicon moulding	Silicon extrusion
Budgeted overheads (£)	450,000	352,520
Budgeted direct labour hours		
Budgeted machine hours		

Task 5.8

Drag and drop the correct entries into the journal below to record the following transactions:

1   Production overheads absorbed into production

2   Indirect labour transferred to production overheads

3   Direct materials issued to production

The choices are:

Debit: Production, Credit: Production overheads

Debit: Production overheads, Credit: Wages

Debit: Inventory, Credit: Production

Debit: Production, Credit: Inventory

Debit: Production, Credit: Finished goods

Debit: Production overheads, Credit: Production

Production overheads absorbed into production		
Indirect labour transferred to production overheads		
Direct materials issued to production		

Task 5.9

Drag and drop the correct entries into the journal below to record the following transactions for overheads:

Transaction 1.   Over-absorbed: absorbed greater than incurred
Transaction 2.   Under-absorbed: incurred greater than absorbed

The drag and drop choices are:

- Debit: production overheads, Credit: statement of profit or loss
- Debit: statement of profit or loss, Credit: production overheads

	Drag and drop choice
Transaction 1	
Transaction 2	

Task 5.10

In JKR Ltd, the overhead for the period was under absorbed.

The accounting entries at the end of a period for production overhead under-absorbed would be (tick the correct boxes):

	Debit	Credit	No entry in this a/c
Overhead control account			
Production account			
Statement of profit or loss			

Chapter 6 – Job, batch and service costing

Task 6.1

Drag and drop the correct entries into the box below to match the correct cost unit to a service:

Full-time student
Meal served
Occupied bed-night
Passenger/kilometre, tonne/kilometre
Patient-day

Service	Cost unit
Road, rail and air transport services	
Hotels	
Education	
Hospitals	
Catering establishments	

Task 6.2

Petra Jones is a builder who has issued a quote for a conservatory. Now the job is completed, she would like you to calculate any variances that have arisen. **State whether each variance is favourable or adverse (unfavourable).** The details are in the table below. Input your answers into the right hand column.

Job number 03456

	Budget £	Actual £	Variance F/A £
Direct materials			
Plasterboard	3,600.00	3,500.00	
Wood and door frames	4,750.00	4,802.00	
Insulation	1,050.00	1,145.00	
Electrical fittings	320.00	300.00	
Windows	2,220.00	2,576.00	
Paint	270.00	250.00	
Direct labour			
Construction	554.00	641.00	
Electrical	224.00	160.00	
	Budget £	Actual £	Variance F/A £
Decorating	165.00	205.00	
Direct expenses			
Hire of specialist lathe	240.00	240.00	

	Budget £	Actual £	Variance F/A £
Overheads (based on direct lab hrs)			
84/90 hours @ £15.00	1,260.00	1,350.00	

Task 6.3

(a) Petra Jones has also asked you to highlight any variances above 5% for further investigation. Use the table below to make your calculations. Enter the percentages to one decimal place.

(b) She also wants you to calculate the profit on the job, comparing this with the original quotation made based on 20% of total cost.

(c) Calculate the percentage variance between the original profit and the final profit figure. Give your answer to 1 decimal place.

	%

	Budget £	Actual £	Variance F/A £	%
Direct materials				
Plasterboard	3,600.00	3,500.00	100F	
Wood and door frames	4,750.00	4,802.00	52A	
Insulation	1,050.00	1,145.00	95A	
Electrical fittings	320.00	300.00	20F	
Windows	2,220.00	2,576.00	356A	
Paint	270.00	250.00	20F	
Direct labour				
Construction	554.00	641.00	87A	
Electrical	224.00	160.00	64F	
Decorating	165.00	205.00	40A	
Direct expenses				
Hire of specialist lathe	240.00	240.00	0	
Overheads (based on direct lab hrs)				
84/90 hours @ £15.00	1,260.00	1,350.00	90A	
Total cost	14,653.00			
Profit	2,930.60			
Net price	17,583.60			
VAT at 20%	3,516.72			
Total price	21,100.32			

Task 6.4

Which of the following are characteristics of service costing?

	✓
High levels of indirect costs as a proportion of total cost	
Cost units are often intangible	
Use of composite cost units	
Use of equivalent units	

Task 6.5

Product Tee is made in batches of 32,000 units and the following costs are estimated.

Product Tee	£ per batch
Direct materials	176,000
Direct labour	230,400
Variable overheads	48,000
Fixed manufacturing overheads	73,600
Fixed administration, selling and distribution costs	54,400
Total costs	582,400

(a)   Calculate the total cost of one unit of product Tee.

£ [   ]

(b)   Calculate the full absorption cost of one unit of product Tee.

£ [   ]

(c)   Calculate the full absorption cost of one batch of product Tee.

£ [   ]

BPP LEARNING MEDIA

Chapter 7 – Standard costing and budgeting

Task 7.1

Are the following statements true or false?

	True ✓	False ✓
A standard cost is a planned unit cost		
Standard costing can be used to value inventory		

Task 7.2

Florrie Ltd makes a product using three different types of material. Each product requires seven kgs of direct material A, four litres of direct material B and three metres of direct material C. Direct material A costs £1 per kg, direct material B costs £2 per litre and direct material C costs £3 per metre.

What are the standard material costs for a single product?

	Standard cost £
Material A	
Material B	
Material C	
Total	

Task 7.3

Are the following statements true or false?

	True ✓	False ✓
Standard material cost per unit = standard material usage x standard material cost per unit of material		
Standard costing can be used as a control device		
Standard costing provides actual future costs		
Standard costing provides information for budgeting		

Task 7.4

CC Ltd manufactures a carbonated drink which is sold in 1 litre bottles. During the bottling process there is a 20% loss of liquid input due to spillage and evaporation. The standard usage of liquid per bottle is:

	✓
0.80 litres	
1.00 litres	
1.20 litres	
1.25 litres	

Task 7.5

Complete the following statement by selecting the correct options to complete the gaps below.

The standard labour cost of a product can be established by multiplying the...	Gap 1	by the...	Gap 2

Gap 1	✓
price per litre	
price per kg	
rate per hour	

Gap 2	✓
number of labour hours per unit	
Total number of units	

Task 7.6

Paris Ltd has prepared a forecast for the next quarter for one of its small components, PA01. This component is produced in batches, and the forecast is based on producing and selling 3,000 batches.

One of the customers of Paris Ltd has indicated that it may be significantly increasing its order level for component PA01 for the next quarter, and it appears that activity levels of 3,750 batches and 5,000 batches are feasible.

The semi-variable costs should be calculated using the high-low method. If 7,500 batches are sold the total semi-variable cost will be £18,450, and there is a constant unit variable cost up to this volume.

Complete the table below and calculate the estimated profit per batch of PA01 at the different activity levels.

Batches produced and sold	3,000	3,750	5,000
	£	£	£
Sales revenue	60,000		
Variable costs:			

BPP LEARNING MEDIA

Batches produced and sold	3,000	3,750	5,000
	£	£	£
Direct materials	5,700		
Direct labour	27,000		
Overheads	9,300		
Semi-variable costs:	9,450		
Variable element			
Fixed element			
Total cost	51,450		
Total profit	8,550		
Profit per batch (to 2 decimal places)	2.85		

Task 7.7

The financial controller at Paris Ltd has just informed you of the following cost increases and asked you to recalculate the budget at the three activity levels.

Direct materials £2.00/kg. 1 kg is used in each PA01.

Direct labour £10/hr. It takes 1 hour to make a PA01.

Overheads are now £3.20 per PA01.

Complete the table below and calculate the estimated profit per batch of PA01 at the different activity levels.

Batches produced and sold	3,000	3,750	5,000
	£	£	£
Sales revenue	60,000		
Variable costs:			
Direct materials			
Direct labour			
Overheads			
Semi-variable costs:	9,450		
Variable element			
Fixed element			
Total cost			
Total profit			
Profit per batch (to 2 decimal places)			

Task 7.8

A customer has put in an order for 4,000 batches. Production is stopped where the profit per batch is less than £2. Recommend to management whether Paris Ltd should go ahead with the order. **Fill in the table below:**

Batches produced and sold	3,000	4,000
	£	£
Sales revenue	60,000	
Variable costs:		
Direct materials	6,000	
Direct labour	30,000	
Overheads	9,600	
Semi-variable costs:		
Variable element	6,000	
Fixed element	3,450	
Total cost	55,050	
Total profit	4,950	
Profit per batch (to 2 decimal places)	1.65	

Choose the correct option below.

Paris Ltd should accept/reject the order for 4,000 units.

Task 7.9

Claridges Ltd has prepared a forecast for the next quarter for one of its small Metal components, the zigger. This component is produced in batches and the forecast is based on selling and producing 3,000 batches.

One of the customers of Claridges Ltd has indicated that it may be significantly increasing its order level for the zigger for the next quarter, and it appears that activity levels of 5,000 batches and 7,000 batches are feasible.

The semi-variable costs should be calculated using the high-low method. If 7,500 batches are sold the total semi-variable cost will be £18,450, and there is a constant unit variable cost up to this volume.

Complete the table below and calculate the estimated profit per batch of the zigger at the different activity levels:

Batches produced and sold	3,000	5,000	7,000
	£	£	£
Sales revenue	90,000		
Variable costs:			
Direct materials	13,500		
Direct labour	31,500		
Overheads	18,000		

Batches produced and sold	3,000	5,000	7,000
	£	£	£
Semi-variable costs:	9,450		
Variable element			
Fixed element			
Total cost	72,450		
Total profit	17,550		
Profit per batch (to 2 decimal places)	5.85		

Task 7.10

CCC Ltd has prepared a forecast for the next quarter for one of its products. The products are produced in batches and the forecast is based on selling and producing 4,000 batches.

The managing director would like to expand the business and is interested to know the profits that could be made if 6,000 batches were made and sold and 9,000 batches were made and sold.

The semi-variable costs should be calculated using the high-low method. If 6,500 batches are sold the total semi-variable cost will be £24,250, and there is a constant unit variable cost up to this volume.

Complete the table below and calculate the estimated profit per batch of the product at the different activity levels:

Batches produced and sold	4,000	6,000	9,000
	£	£	£
Sales revenue	140,000		
Variable costs:			
Direct materials	22,000		
Direct labour	50,000		
Overheads	28,000		
Semi-variable costs:	16,750		
Total cost	116,750		
Total profit	23,250		
Profit per batch (to 2 decimal places)	5.81		

Task 7.11

Are the following statements true or false?

	True ✓	False ✓
A fixed budget can never be changed		
A rolling budget is continually updated		
A rolling budget allows a more accurate budget to be produced		

BPP LEARNING MEDIA

Chapter 8 – Variance analysis

Task 8.1

Paris Ltd has the following original budget and actual performance for product SHEP for the year ending 30 September:

	Budget	Actual
Volume sold	150,000	156,000
	£000	£000
Sales revenue	1,200	1,326
Less costs:		
Direct materials	375	372
Direct labour	450	444
Overheads	225	250
Operating profit	150	260

Both direct materials and direct labour are variable costs, but the overheads are fixed.

Complete the table below to show a flexed budget and the resulting variances against this budget for the year. Show the actual variance amount for sales, each cost, and operating profit, in the column headed 'Variance' and indicate whether this is Favourable or Adverse by entering F or A in the final column. If neither F nor A enter 0.

	Flexed Budget	Actual	Variance	Favourable F or Adverse A
Volume sold		156,000		
	£000	£000	£000	
Sales revenue		1,326		
Less costs:				
Direct materials		372		
Direct labour		444		
Overheads		250		
Operating profit		260		

Task 8.2

The Managing Director of Paris Ltd has asked you to explain why the actual outcome was better than budgeted. He wants you to do some calculations and suggest reasons why the revenues and costs may be better than budgeted.

Input your calculations to two decimal places into the table below, in the two right hand columns. Ignore overheads.

	Flexed Budget	Actual	Budget unit cost/revenue	Actual unit cost/revenue
Volume sold	156,000	156,000		
	£000	£000		
Sales revenue	1,248	1,326		
Less costs:				
Direct materials	390	372		
Direct labour	468	444		
Overheads	225	250		
Operating profit	165	260		

Are the following true or false?

The unit selling price difference may be due to a rise in the sales price not planned in the budget.	True/False
The unit selling price difference may be due to fewer bulk discounts to customers	True/False
The materials unit price difference may be due to bulk buying discounts.	True/False
The materials unit price difference may be due to a cheaper source of supply.	True/False
The labour cost difference may be due to having more lower paid employees.	True/False
The labour cost difference may be due to efficiency savings.	True/False

Task 8.3

Balloonz Ltd had budgeted to manufacture and sell 40,000 packets of balloons last year. However, due to a shortage of staff, it was only able to manufacture and sell 32,000 packets. Balloonz Ltd's manufacturing costs are all variable except for fixed overheads.

Complete the table below to show a flexed budget and the resulting variances against the budget for the year. Show the actual variance amount for sales revenue and each cost in the column headed 'Variance'.

Note:

- Adverse variances must be denoted with a minus sign or brackets.
- Enter 0 where any figure is zero.

	Original budget	Flexed budget	Actual	Variance
Number of packets	40,000	32,000	32,000	
	£	£	£	£
Sales revenue	130,000		96,000	
Less costs:				
Direct materials and direct labour	48,000		36,800	
Variable overheads	22,000		19,200	
Fixed overheads	14,200		13,600	
Profit from operations	45,800		26,400	

Task 8.4

Pumpken Ltd had budgeted to manufacture and sell 60,000 books in May. However, due to some bad publicity, it was only able to manufacture and sell 45,000 books. Pumpken's manufacturing costs are all variable except for fixed overheads.

Complete the table below to show a flexed budget and the resulting variances against the budget for May. Show the actual variance amount for sales revenue and each cost in the column headed 'Variance'.

Note:

- Adverse variances must be denoted with a minus sign or brackets.
- Enter 0 where any figure is zero.

	Original budget	Flexed budget	Actual	Variance
Number of books	60,000	45,000	45,000	
	£	£	£	£
Sales revenue	1,140,000		910,200	
Less costs:				
Direct materials and direct labour	480,000		375,000	
Variable overheads	540,000		406,400	
Fixed overheads	56,000		55,000	
Profit from operations	64,000		73,800	

Task 8.5

Fissie Drinks Ltd had budgeted to manufacture and sell 30,000 cans of pop in January. However, due to a health scare in the media about pop, it was only able to manufacture and sell 25,000 cans. Fissie Drinks Ltd's manufacturing costs are all variable except for fixed overheads.

(a) Complete the table below to show a flexed budget and the resulting variances against the budget for January. Show the actual variance amount for sales revenue and each cost in the column headed 'Variance'.

Note:

- Adverse variances must be denoted with a minus sign or brackets.
- Enter 0 where any figure is zero.

	Original budget	Flexed budget	Actual	Variance
Number of cans	30,000	25,000	25,000	
	£	£	£	£
Sales revenue	22,500		18,000	
Less costs:				
Direct materials and direct labour	10,500		8,500	
Variable overheads	6,000		4,200	
Fixed overheads	4,000		4,100	
Profit from operations	2,000		1,200	

(b) Referring to your answer for part (a), which one of the variances has had the greatest impact in increasing the profit from operations?

	✓
Sales revenue	
Direct materials and direct labour	
Variable overheads	
Fixed overheads	

(c) Which one of the following might have caused the variance for direct materials and direct labour costs?

	✓
A decrease in material prices	
An increase in employees' pay	
An increase in material prices	
Less efficient usage of direct labour	

Chapter 9 – Marginal costing

Task 9.1

Paris Ltd uses absorption costing, but is looking at adopting marginal costing across some of its products. The details for the PA121 are below:

Direct materials	£8.50
Direct labour	£17.00
Variable overheads	£3.00
Fixed overheads	£850,000

Overheads are absorbed on the machine hour basis, and it is estimated that in the next accounting period machine hours will total 250,000. Each unit requires two hours of machine time.

What is the cost per unit using:

(a)   Absorption costing
(b)   Marginal costing?

Task 9.2

Drag and drop the correct answer into the sentence below:

Less for absorption costing

More for absorption costing

The same for both types of costing

In the long run, total profit for a company will be ⬚ whether marginal costing or absorption costing is used.

Task 9.3

Drag and drop the correct answer into the sentence below:

Absorption costing, marginal costing

Marginal costing, absorption costing

It might be argued that ⬚ is preferable to ⬚ in management accounting, in order to be consistent with the requirement of current accounting standards and financial reporting.

Task 9.4

Cost and selling price details for product Z are as follows.

	£
Direct materials	6.00
Direct labour	7.50
Variable overhead	2.50
Fixed overhead absorption rate	5.00
	21.00
Profit	9.00
Selling price	30.00

Budgeted production for the month was 5,000 units although the company managed to produce 5,800 units, selling 5,200 of them and incurring fixed overhead costs of £27,400.

(a)   What was the marginal costing profit for the month?

	✓
£45,400	
£46,800	
£53,800	
£72,800	

(b)   What was the absorption costing profit for the month?

	✓
£45,200	
£45,400	
£46,800	
£48,400	

BPP LEARNING MEDIA

Task 9.5

Product Dee is made in batches of 16,000 units and the following costs are estimated.

Product Dee	£ per batch
Direct materials	176,000
Direct labour	230,400
Variable overheads	48,000
Fixed manufacturing overheads	73,600
Fixed administration, selling and distribution costs	54,400
Total costs	582,400

(a)   Calculate the total cost of one unit of product Dee.

£ [   ]

(b)   Calculate the full absorption cost of one unit of product Dee.

£ [   ]

(c)   Calculate the full absorption cost of one batch of product Dee.

£ [   ]

(d)   Calculate the marginal cost of one batch of product Dee.

£ [   ]

(e)   Calculate the marginal cost of one unit of product Dee.

£ [   ]

Chapter 10 – Short-term decision-making

Task 10.1

The COLIN has a selling price of £22 per unit with a total variable cost of £17 per unit. Paris Ltd estimates that the fixed costs per quarter associated with this product are £45,000.

(a) Calculate the budgeted breakeven, in units, for product COLIN.

| | units

(b) Calculate the budgeted breakeven sales, in £s, for product COLIN.

£ | |

(c) Complete the table below to show the budgeted margin of safety in units and the margin of safety percentage (to the nearest whole %) and the margin of safety in revenue if Paris Ltd sells 9,500 units or 10,500 units of product COLIN.

Units of COLIN sold	9,500	10,500
Margin of safety (units)		
Margin of safety percentage		
Margin of safety revenue		

(d) If Paris Ltd wishes to make a profit of £20,000, how many units of COLIN must it sell?

| | units

(e) If Paris Ltd increases the selling price of COLIN by £1 what will be the impact on the breakeven point and the margin of safety, assuming no change in the number of units sold?

	✓
The breakeven point will decrease and the margin of safety will increase.	
The margin of safety will stay the same but the breakeven point will increase.	
The breakeven point will decrease and the margin of safety will stay the same.	
The margin of safety will decrease and the breakeven point will decrease.	

Task 10.2

(a) Paris Ltd has decided to limit the production of the COLIN to 8,000 units per quarter. If the selling price and variable costs remain the same, what is the maximum fixed costs per quarter to breakeven? Remember the selling price is £22 per unit and the variable cost is £17 per unit.

(b) Calculate the revised budgeted breakeven, in £s, for product COLIN if fixed costs are £30,000 per quarter.

£ | |

(c) Complete the table below to show the budgeted margin of safety in units and the margin of safety percentage (to the nearest whole %) if Paris Ltd sells 6,500 units or 7,000 units of product COLIN. Base this on your answer in part (b).

Units of COLIN sold	6,500 £	7,000 £
Margin of safety (units)		
Margin of safety percentage		

(d) If Paris Ltd wishes to make a profit of £10,000, how many units of COLIN must it sell? Is it possible to make this level of profit? Base this on the data in parts (a), (b) and (c).

[   ] units

Task 10.3

A company makes a single product and incurs fixed costs of £30,000 per month. Variable cost per unit is £5 and each unit sells for £15. Monthly sales demand is 7,000 units.

The breakeven point in terms of monthly sales units is:

	✓
2,000 units	
3,000 units	
4,000 units	
6,000 units	

Task 10.4

A company manufactures a single product for which cost and selling price data are as follows.

Selling price per unit	£12
Variable cost per unit	£8
Fixed costs per month	£96,000
Budgeted monthly sales	30,000 units

The margin of safety, expressed as a percentage of budgeted monthly sales, is (to the nearest whole number):

	✓
20%	
25%	
73%	
125%	

Task 10.5

Information concerning K Co's single product is as follows.

	£ per unit
Selling price	6.00
Variable production cost	1.20
Variable selling cost	0.40
Fixed production cost	4.00
Fixed selling cost	0.80

Budgeted production and sales for the year are 10,000 units.

(a) What is the company's breakeven point, to the nearest whole unit?

	✓
8,000 units	
8,333 units	
10,000 units	
10,909 units	

(b) How many units must be sold if K Co wants to achieve a profit of £11,000 for the year?

	✓
2,500 units	
9,833 units	
10,625 units	
13,409 units	

Task 10.6

Bluetop Ltd is reviewing two contracts, Top4 and Top5, for next month. The contracts will require a specialist grade of material. The following forecasts have been prepared:

Forecast	Top4	Top5	Total
Contribution (£)	18,000	13,500	31,500
Fixed costs (£)	5,000	5,000	10,000
Profit from operations (£)	13,000	8,500	21,500
Number of units	3,000	1,500	
Total specialist material required (kg)	1,125	750	

There is a shortage of specialist material for next month due to a supplier shortage.

This means that only 1,125 kg of specialist material is expected to be available for these two contracts.

(a) Complete all cells in the forecast profit statement below to recommend how many units should be produced under each contract, and the forecast profit/loss made.

Forecast	Top4	Top5	Total
Contribution per unit (£)			
Contribution per kg (£)			
Ranking			
Total material available (kg)			
Material allocated (kg)			
Number of units produced			
Total contribution earned (£)			
Less: fixed costs (£)			
Forecast profit/loss made (£)			

(b) Complete the following sentence, using your results from (a) above.

Contract Top5 [   ] ▼ be selected as the first contract to produce next month as it has the highest [   ] ▼ .

Picklist:

should
should not
contribution per unit
contribution per kg used

Task 10.7

Golden Ltd is reviewing two contracts, Sun and Rain, for next month. The contracts will require a specialist grade of labour. The following forecasts have been prepared:

Forecast	Sun	Rain
Contribution (£)	9,000	6,000
Fixed costs (£)	3,500	3,500
Profit from operations (£)	5,500	2,500
Number of units	3,000	1,500
Total specialist labour hours required (hours)	2,250	3,000

There is a shortage of specialist labour for next month due to staff holidays.

This means that only 5,000 hours of specialist labour are expected to be available for these two contracts.

Complete all cells in the forecast profit statement below to recommend how many units should be produced under each contract, and the forecast profit/loss made.

Forecast	Sun	Rain	Total
Contribution per unit (£)			
Contribution per hour (£)			
Ranking			
Total labour hours available (hours)			
Labour hours allocated (hours)			
Number of units produced			
Total contribution earned (£)			
Less: fixed costs (£)			
Forecast profit/loss made (£)			

Chapter 11 – Cash management

Task 11.1

Complete the following statement by selecting the correct options to complete the gaps below.

The working capital operating cycle is the...	Gap 1	Liquid assets include...	Gap 2

Gap 1	✓
period between cash being paid for purchases and cash received for sales	
inventory holding period plus trade receivables' collection period less trade payables' payment period	

Gap 2	✓
Non-current assets	
Cash, receivables and inventory	

Task 11.2

Kitten Ltd buys raw materials on three months' credit, holds them in store for four months and then issues them to production. The production cycle is a couple of days, and then finished goods are held for one month before they are sold. Credit customers are normally allowed two months' credit.

What is Kitten Ltd's approximate working capital cycle in months?

1 month ☐

2 months ☐

3 months ☐

4 months ☐

Task 11.3

During the year ending 30 June a business had a working capital cycle of 87 days. It had a trade receivables' collection period of 77 days and trade payables' payment period of 41 days.

What is the inventory holding period of the business, in days?

31 days ☐

36 days ☐

46 days ☐

51 days ☐

Task 11.4

A business has a working capital cycle of 76 days. This is based on an inventory holding period of 65 days, trade receivables' collection period of 55 days and trade payables' payment period of 44 days. The Finance Director of the business wants to improve this.

Which of the following will have the effect of shortening the working capital cycle of the business?

Taking advantage of early settlement discounts offered by suppliers ☐

Offering an early settlement discount to customers ☐

Increasing the cash balance held in the business's current account ☐

Increasing the credit terms offered to customers from 30 days to 60 days ☐

Task 11.5

The carrying amount of non-current assets on 1 January was £125,000 and the statement of financial position at 31 December shows non-current assets of £152,000. During the year £12,500 depreciation was charged. There were no non-current asset disposals.

What was the cash paid to acquire non-current assets in the year ended 31 December?

£12,500 ☐

£14,500 ☐

£27,000 ☐

£39,500 ☐

Task 11.6

A business decides to sell one of its machines. The machine being sold originally cost £64,400. At the date of disposal, accumulated depreciation on the machine amounts to £38,640. The machine is sold for £23,800.

What was the profit or loss on disposal of the machine?

£1,960 profit ☐

£1,960 loss ☐

£14,840 profit ☐

£14,840 loss ☐

Task 11.7

Which of the following statements about working capital (WC) is correct?

	✓
WC is the difference between a company's total assets and its total liabilities	
WC is the difference between a company's total assets and its current liabilities	
WC is the difference between a company's current assets and its total liabilities	
WC is the difference between a company's current assets and its current liabilities	

Task 11.8

Which of the following is not classed as working capital?

	✓
Overdraft	
Inventory	
Accruals	
Bank loan	

Task 11.9

A manufacturing company is preparing its cash budget for the three months ending 31 July. The production budget is estimated to be as follows.

	April	May	June	July	August
Production quantity (units)	1,020	1,220	1,320	1,520	1,620

The materials required for the product are 2 kg per unit costing £40 per kg and are purchased in the month prior to production and paid for in the following month. At 1 April there are 550 kgs of raw material in inventory but these are to be reduced by 50 kgs per month for each of the next four months.

(a)   Use the table below to complete the purchases budget in kgs and £s for April to July

	April Kgs	May Kgs	June Kgs	July Kgs
Materials required for production				
April				
May				
June				
July				

BPP
LEARNING
MEDIA

	April Kgs	May Kgs	June Kgs	July Kgs
Opening inventory				
Closing inventory				
Purchases in kgs				

Cost of material purchases	April £	May £	June £	July £
April				
May				
June				
July				

(b)   Calculate the cash payments to suppliers for May to July

	May £	June £	July £
Cash payments			

Task 11.10

A business manufactures and sells a single product, each unit of which requires 20 minutes of labour. The wage rate is £8.40 per hour. The sales budget is anticipated to be:

	April	May	June	July
Sales in units	7,200	7,050	6,450	6,000

The product is produced one month prior to sale and wages are paid in the month of production.

Calculate the cash payments for wages for each of the three months from April to June.

Labour budget – hours	April Hours	May Hours	June Hours
April			
May			
June			

Cash payment for wages – £	April £	May £	June £
April			
May			
June			

Chapter 12 – Spreadsheets

Task 12.1

You have been given a spreadsheet **FinanceTeam.xls** which shows qualification details of members of the finance team at ABC co. It contains two worksheets: 'Finance Team' and 'Subs'.

Download this spreadsheet file from www.bpp.com/aatspreadsheets and save in the appropriate location. Rename it using the following format: **'your initial-surname-AAT no –dd.mm.yy-Task12.1'**.

For example: J-Donnovan-123456-12.03xx-Task12.1

A **high degree of accuracy** is required. You **must save your work as an .XLS or .XLSX file** at regular intervals to avoid losing your work.

(a)   Open the renamed spreadsheet and open the subs worksheet.

     •   Format the data on this page as a table, include the headings.

     •   On the finance team worksheet, use a LOOKUP function to complete the subs column.

     •   Format the subs figures in a red font colour.

ABC company offers free health check-ups to all employees aged 40 or older.

(b)   Use conditional formatting to highlight all employees aged 40 and over.

     •   Sort the data based on employee number, from lowest to highest.

ABC company employees are given 24 days of holiday per year. When they have served at the company for 5 or more years, they receive an additional 5 days leave per year.

(c)   Rename column J as 'holiday'.

     •   Use an IF statement to complete the data in this column to show how many days holiday per year to which each individual is entitled.

(d)   Format the data as a table with light blue shading.

     •   Use the filter function to display only individuals who are members or students of the AAT who have not yet paid their subs.

Task 12.2

You have been given a spreadsheet **Orders.xls** which shows an extract of a spreadsheet of purchases made by various departments in the organisation. It contains one worksheet: Sheet 1.

Download this spreadsheet file from www.bpp.com/aatspreadsheets and save in the appropriate location. Rename it using the following format: **'your initial-surname-AAT no –dd.mm.yy-Task12.2'**.

For example: J-Donnovan-123456-12.03xx-Task12.2

A **high degree of accuracy** is required. You **must save your work as an .XLS or .XLSX file** at regular intervals to avoid losing your work.

Since this spreadsheet was prepared, the company 'Cater Co' has been rebranded and the name of the company has changed to 'Corporate Catering Company'.

(a)   Open the renamed spreadsheet.

     •   Use find and replace to update any cells which refer to 'Cater co' to show the new name of the company.

     •   Rename the worksheet 'order list'.

(b)   Create a pivot table and pivot chart in a new worksheet to represent the amount spent with each supplier.

- Rename the chart as 'Spend per supplier'.

- Rename the worksheet 'Supplier spend' and ensure the order of the worksheets is such that the order list worksheet is on the left and the supplier spend worksheet is on the right.

(c)   Return to the Order List worksheet and format the data as a table using data style medium 14.

(d)   Select the entire worksheet, copy the contents and paste this into a new worksheet.

- Rename the new worksheet 'Sales team order summary'.

- Apply filters to the data to show only data relating to orders raised by the sales team.

(e)   Merge cells A1:E1 and add the text 'Sales Department Order Summary'.

- Change the font size in the merged cell to 16 and centre the text.

- Use the fill function to make the merged cell dark green and change the font colour in this cell to white.

- Remove the gridlines.

(f)   Prepare the document for being sent to the sales team. It is important that the sales team can see only their worksheet and none of the workings or data for the other departments.

- Hide the worksheets 'Order list' and 'Supplier Spend'.

- Protect the workbook so that no changes can be made to the source data and the hidden sheets remain hidden (greyed out if attempt to unhide).

- Use the SaveAs feature to save a copy of this version of the spreadsheet called 'Sales Team Order Summary'.

Task 12.3

You have been given a spreadsheet **Timesheet.xls** which is used by employees of ABC Co. to record the hours they have worked and where they have spent their time. Your spreadsheet currently contains one worksheet: Week 1. This contains details of the time spent by one employee, Harrison, during that week.

Download this spreadsheet file from www.bpp.com/aatspreadsheets and save in the appropriate location. Rename it using the following format: **'your initial-surname-AAT no –dd.mm.yy-Task12.3'**.

For example: J-Donnovan-123456-12.03xx-Task12.3

A **high degree of accuracy** is required. You **must save your work as an .XLS or .XLSX file** at regular intervals to avoid losing your work.

ABC company operates a flexitime system. It counts one working day to be 7.5 hours long. However, employees can work more or fewer hours in any given day, so long as the time is made up elsewhere. If employees accumulate 7.5 hours of flexitime, they can choose to take a 'flexi-day'. A flexi-day is a day off in lieu of the time that has been worked to accumulate these hours and, from the employees' point of view, works like an additional day of annual leave.

(a) Open the renamed spreadsheet.

- Add a formula to cell C30 to calculate the amount of flexi-time earned or used on Monday. Apply this formula to the rest of the days of the week.

- Add a formula to cell C31 to calculate the current balance of flexitime on Monday. Apply this formula to the rest of the days of the week.

- Insert formulas in cells I25 and I28 with robust formulas to check for errors in the summing of data.

As part of the flexi-time system, employees are not allowed to work for less than six hours in any given day.

(b) Use a data validation function in cells C28:G28 to identify any days where less than six hours are worked.

- Set the data validation to circle in red any days where fewer than six hours have been worked.

Employees are also not allowed to charge more than two hours to the admin account in any given day.

(c) Use a data validation function to prevent more than two hours of admin being charged on any given day.

- Attempt to change the admin charge on Monday to three hours.

You are given the following information about Harrison's working patterns for the following two weeks:

In week two, Harrison was on annual leave all five days.

In week three, Harrison attended a training course for 8 hours on both Monday and Tuesday. On Wednesday he charged 3 hours to each of projects 1 and 2 and 2 hours to admin. On Thursday he charged 4 hours to project 1, 3 hours to supervision and 2 hours to admin. On Friday he charged 7 hours to project 3 and one hour to admin.

(d) Insert two new worksheets.

- Change the name of the new worksheets to 'Week 2' and 'Week 3'.

- Copy the format and formulas used on Week 1 to Week 2 and Week 3 and populate the spreadsheets with the information given above.

- Link the formula related to flexi-time to ensure the balance from Week 1 is carried over to week 2 and so on.

(e) Insert a new worksheet and rename it 'Summary'.

- Use the data from Weeks 1–3 to produce a summary sheet which collates the total number of hours charged to each activity per week.

- Format the summary sheet in the same style as the weekly worksheets.

- Use the split function to keep the header rows in place.

Task 12.4

You have been given a spreadsheet **Sickness.xls** which shows an extract from a record of employee sick leave taken. It contains two worksheets: 'Record' and 'Employee names'.

Download this spreadsheet file from www.bpp.com/aatspreadsheets and save in the appropriate location. Rename it using the following format: **'your initial-surname-AAT no –dd.mm.yy-Task12.4'**.

For example: J-Donnovan-123456-12.03xx-Task12.4

BPP
LEARNING
MEDIA

A **high degree of accuracy** is required. You **must save your work as an .XLS or .XLSX file** at regular intervals to avoid losing your work.

(a)   Open the renamed spreadsheet and go into the Record tab.

- Use a lookup function to complete the employee name column.

Sickness certificates from a medical professional are required in order to verify any sickness period in excess of 5 days.

(b)   Use an IF statement in Column I along with a lookup function in Column E to determine whether or not a certificate is required.

- The IF statement should return the values 0 for no and 1 for yes and the lookup should refer to the table in Columns J and K.

- Hide Columns I, J and K.

Employees should not take more than 15 sickness days in total per year.

(c)   Insert a pivot table on a new worksheet which summarises the total number of sickness days taken by each employee.

- Rename this worksheet 'Summary'.

Employees are a cause for concern for the organisation if they take frequent short periods of sickness.

(d)   Return to the 'Record' worksheet and sort the data by employee number.

- Use a subtotal function to count the instances of sickness taken by each individual.

- Highlight the entire worksheet and apply conditional formatting to highlight the employee number of any individuals who are at risk of falling into the frequent sickness category.

Task 12.5

You have been given a spreadsheet **TestResults.xls** which shows scores achieved by students in four tests and an overall score. It contains one worksheet: 'Test Results'.

Download this spreadsheet file from www.bpp.com/aatspreadsheets and save in the appropriate location. Rename it using the following format: **'your initial-surname-AAT no –dd.mm.yy-Task12.5'**.

For example: J-Donnovan-123456-12.03xx-Task12.5

A **high degree of accuracy** is required. You **must save your work as an .XLS or .XLSX file** at regular intervals to avoid losing your work.

(a)   Open the renamed spreadsheet.

- Run a data validation test to remove any duplicate entries.

(b)   Prepare a histogram based on the overall scores achieved by the students.

- The bins used should be in intervals of 10, beginning with 100.
- Change the axis to 'No. students' and 'total score'.
- Change the title of the histogram to 'Overall score analysis'.

Students who have scored over 140 are considered suitable candidates for a scholarship. The five highest scoring students will automatically gain a place in the scholarship program. There are ten places available. The remaining students who fall into this category will be offered an interview for this program.

(c) Return to worksheet 'test results' and format the data as a table using table style medium 12.

- Use the filters within the table to identify only those students who will be offered an interview for the scholarship program.

- Reorder the data using the filter to rank the potential scholarship candidates from highest scoring to lowest scoring.

(d) Add a column called 'outcome' in Column H.

- Insert the text 'Scholarship' in this column next to the top 5 students, and Interview against the remaining students.

- Remove the filters, and then refilter to show only students who are below average.

- Add the text Refer in the outcome box for these students.

- Remove the filters.

- Filter using the outcome filter to identify all students who have passed the tests but who are not contenders for the scholarship program.

(e) Password protect the entire workbook using the password Test123.

Task 12.6

You work for Williams restaurant, a large city centre restaurant.

You cover all aspects of bookkeeping and accounting for the business.

In the quarter to 31 March 20X5, the restaurant budgeted to serve 4,500 meals (each budgeted meal consists of an average food and drink cost based on previous customer behaviour). However the restaurant only served 3,825 meals in the quarter to 31 March 20X5.

Download the spreadsheet file "Task 12.6 Williams.xlsx" from www.bpp.com/aatspreadsheets. Save the spreadsheet file in the appropriate location and rename it in the following format: 'your initial-surname-AAT no-dd.mm.yy-Task12.6'. For example: H-Darch-123456-12.03.xx-Task12.6

A **high degree of accuracy** is required. You must **save your work as an .XLS or.XLSX file** at regular intervals to avoid losing your work.

(a) Open this renamed file. Calculate the percentage to flex this budget in line with the information about meals sold and insert this percentage figure into cell D1.

(b) Format cell D1 to be in italics.

(c) In column D calculate the flexed budget for the relevant entries using absolute referencing where appropriate.

(d) Calculate the variances for each revenue and each cost. Show these in Column F. Show adverse variances as negative figures with a minus sign.

(e) In cell A15 insert the title 'Operating profit'. Calculate the operating profit for the original budget, flexed budget and actual results.

(f) Calculate the overall variance in cell F15.

(g) Copy the range A3 to F14 and paste into cell A19.

(h) Delete row 20 which contains the revenue figures.

(i) Produce subtotals for each of: consumables, labour, variable overheads and fixed overheads.

(j) Show subtotals in original budget, flexed budget, actual results and variances columns.

(k) Hide the detail to only show the subtotals and a grand total, not the individual components.

BPP LEARNING MEDIA

Task 12.7

You are a part-qualified accounting technician. You work for Westside Hospital.

You cover all aspects of bookkeeping and accounting for the hospital.

The hospital receives £180 per patient day from the government. It has some variable and fixed costs. Some of its staffing costs are stepped fixed costs, which are dependent on patient days. Its staffing costs are as follows:

Patient days per annum	Supervisors	Nurses	Assistants
Up to 20,000	5	8	22
20,000 – 24,000	5	10	26
Over 24,000	5	12	30

The salary for each supervisor is £30,000 each, nurse £23,000, assistant £16,000.

For the year ended 31 May 20X6 the hospital budgeted for 19,000 patient days, but there were actually 21,850 patient days.

Westside Hospital intends to open a new wing in May 20X7, which will allow it to accommodate more patients. For the year ended 31 May 20X8 it plans to budget for 25,000 patient days. However the government has indicated that its total funding will be capped at £4 million.

Download the spreadsheet file "Task 12.7 Westside Hospital.xlsx" from www.bpp.com/aatspreadsheets. Save the spreadsheet file in the appropriate location and rename it in the following format: 'your initial-surname-AAT no-dd.mm.yy-Task12.7'. For example: H-Darch-123456-12.03.xx-Task12.7

A **high degree of accuracy** is required. You must **save your work as an .XLS or.XLSX file** at regular intervals to avoid losing your work.

(a)   Open this renamed file. Calculate the percentage to flex the variable costs in this budget in line with the information about patient days and insert this percentage figure into cell D1.

(b)   Centre-align cell D1.

(c)   In cell D3 enter the title 'Flexed budget'. Use the information given above and appropriate formulas to calculate the flexed budget in column D. Format these cells to use commas to show thousands.

(d)   In cell E3 enter the title 'Actual results'. Use a lookup formula to look up the actual results from the 'Information' worksheet into the correct positions in Column E on the 'Question' worksheet.

(e)   In cell F3 insert the title 'Variances'. Calculate the variances for each revenue and each cost. Show these in Column F. Show all figures as positive numbers.

(f)   In cell A15 insert the title 'Surplus/(Deficit)'. Calculate the surplus or deficit income for the original, flexed budget and actual results.

(g)   Calculate the overall variance in cell F15.

(h)   In cell G3 insert the title 'Adverse/Favourable'. Indicate whether each variance is adverse or favourable by inserting 'A' or 'F' in column G.

(i)   Format row 3 to be bold and underlined.

(j)   In cell A17, insert a 2D column chart showing the flexed budget and actual results for each cost.

(k)   Add a legend at the bottom of the chart to identify the columns.

Task 12.8

You are a part-qualified accounting technician.

Download the spreadsheet file "Task 12.8 Farrell.xlsx" from www.bpp.com/aatspreadsheets. Save the spreadsheet file in the appropriate location and rename it in the following format: 'your initial-surname-AAT no-dd.mm.yy-Task12.8'. For example: H-Darch-123456-12.03.xx-Task12.8

A **high degree of accuracy** is required. You must **save your work as an .XLS or.XLSX file** at regular intervals to avoid losing your work.

(a)   Open this renamed file and complete the following in the 'Flexed budget' worksheet.

In the 'Master budget' worksheet, you have been given the original budget which was based on 15,000 annual chargeable consultant hours.

In the 'Actual results' worksheet, you have been given the actual results for the year. Actual chargeable consultant hours were 16,500.

   (i)   Copy the relevant cells from the 'Master budget' and 'Actual results' worksheets into the 'Flexed budget' worksheet in columns C and D (from cell C5 to cell D13).

   (ii)   Calculate the percentage to flex this budget in line with the information above and insert this percentage figure into cell E1. Format this cell to be a percentage with bold font and centre-aligned.

   (iii)   Calculate the flexed budget for the relevant entries using absolute referencing where appropriate. Chow these in column E (from cell E5 to cell E13).

   (iv)   In cell A14 insert the title 'Operating profit'.

   (v)   In cells C14, D14 and E14, use an appropriate formula to calculate the operating profit for the original budget, flexed budget and actual results.

   (vi)   In column F (from cell F5 to cell F13), use an appropriate formula to calculate the variances in £ for revenue and each cost. Adverse variances should be shown as negative.

   (vii)   In cell F14, use an appropriate formula to calculate the overall variance in £.

   (viii) In column G (from cell G5 to cell G13) use an appropriate formula to calculate the variances as a percentage for revenue and each cost. Adverse variances should be shown as negative. Format these cells to show percentages to 1 decimal place.

   (ix)   In cell G14, use an appropriate formula to calculate the overall variance in %. Format this cell to show a percentages to 1 decimal place.

   (x)   In the 'Variance %' column, highlight the three largest negative variances in bold red font.

(b)   Complete the following in the 'Chart' worksheet.

   (i)   Change the chart type to a 2D bar chart.
   (ii)   Add a data table with no legend keys to the chart.
   (iii)   Add a chart title above the chart and label this 'Variances'.

Task 12.9

You are a part-qualified accounting technician. You work for Carter Co, a company that manufactures chairs for the home.

You cover all aspects of bookkeeping and accounting for the business.

The production department has informed you that Carter Co sold 11,500 chairs in the quarter to 30 June 20X8. You are to prepare budgets based on the actual activity level. The original budget was prepared on the assumption of making and selling 10,000 chairs.

BPP
LEARNING
MEDIA

Download the spreadsheet file "Task 12.9.xlsx" from www.bpp.com/aatspreadsheets. Save the spreadsheet file in the appropriate location and rename it in the following format: 'your initial-surname-AAT no-dd.mm.yy-Task12.9'. For example: H-Darch-123456-12.03.xx-Task12.9

A **high degree of accuracy** is required. You must **save your work as an .XLS or.XLSX file** at regular intervals to avoid losing your work.

(a)   Open this renamed file. In the Question worksheet, calculate the percentage to flex the original budget in line with sales being 11,500 and insert this percentage figure into cell D1.

(b)   In cell D3 enter the title 'Flexed budget 11,500'. Calculate the flexed budget for the relevant entries using absolute referencing where appropriate.

(c)   In cell E3 enter the title 'Actual results'. Use copy and paste to take the actual results from the 'Information' worksheet into the correct positions in Column E on the 'Question' worksheet.

(d)   In cell F3 insert the title 'Variances 11,500'. Calculate the variances for each revenue and each cost. Show these in Column F. Show adverse variances as negative numbers.

(e)   In cell A15 insert the title 'Operating profit'. Calculate the operating profit for the original budget, flexed budget and actual results.

(f)   Calculate the overall variance for 11,500 units in cell F15.

(g)   Use conditional formatting in Column F to show all favourable variances in green font and adverse variances in red font.

(h)   In cell F17 use a countif statement to count the number of revenue and cost variances which are adverse.

(i)   Format row 3 to be bold and wrap text.

(j)   In the section of the worksheet labelled 'Carter Co Overhead summary for the quarter ended 30 June 20X8', copy and paste the column headers in cells C3–F3 into cells C20–F20.

(k)   Under each header use a sumif formula to calculate subtotals for each category of costs (Materials, Direct labour, Variable overheads and Fixed overheads) and use an appropriate formula to calculate total costs in row 25.

Task 12.10

You are a part-qualified accounting technician. You work for Trent Co, which manufactures garden barbecues.

You cover all aspects of bookkeeping and accounting for the business.

You have been asked to perform some breakeven analysis based on the budgeted figures for the next 12 months. Forecast sales are 25,000 units and sales price is £60.

Cost figures are as follows:

	£
Direct materials	500,000
Direct labour	350,000
Assembly	200,000
Packaging	280,000

40% of assembly costs and 25% of packaging costs are variable.

The company's target margin of safety is 20% and its target profit is £180,000.

Download the spreadsheet file "Task 12.10.xlsx" from www.bpp.com/aatspreadsheets. Save the spreadsheet file in the appropriate location and rename it in the following format: 'your initial-surname-AAT no-dd.mm.yy-Task12.10. For example: H-Darch-123456-12.03.xx-Task12.10

A **high degree of accuracy** is required. You must **save your work as an .XLS or.XLSX file** at regular intervals to avoid losing your work.

(a)   Open the renamed file. Calculate total revenue and enter it in cell B2.

(b)   Enter total direct materials in cell B4 and total direct labour in cell B5.

(c)   Calculate variable assembly and packaging costs and enter them in cells B6 and B7.

(d)   Calculate total variable costs and enter them in cell B8.

(e)   Calculate variable costs per unit, using the budgeted sales volume of 25,000, and enter it in cell B9.

(f)   Calculate contribution per unit, using the budgeted sales price of £60, and enter it in cell B10.

(g)   Calculate fixed assembly and packaging costs and enter them in cells B12 and B13.

(h)   Calculate total fixed costs and enter them in cell B14.

(i)   Calculate the breakeven point in units and enter it in cell B15. Use conditional formatting to show this figure in green if it is less than the budgeted sales volume and red if it is more than the budgeted sales volume.

(j)   Calculate the breakeven point in revenue terms and enter it in cell B16.

(k)   Calculate the contribution/sales ratio and enter it in cell B17, showing it to 2 decimal places.

(l)   Calculate the margin of safety in units and enter it in cell B18.

(m)   Calculate the margin of safety in % terms and enter it in cell B19, showing it to 2 decimal places. Highlight this figure with a yellow background and black border. Put an IF statement in cell C19 to show HIGHER if it is greater than the target margin of safety of 20%, LOWER if it is less than the target margin of safety.

(n)   Calculate the volume of sales needed to achieve the target profit of £180,000 and enter it in cell B20. Highlight this figure with a yellow background and black border. Put an IF statement in cell C20 to show LESS if the budgeted sales volume of 25,000 units is lower than the volume of sales needed to achieve the target profit, MORE if the budgeted sales volume Is higher.

BPP
LEARNING
MEDIA

Answers

BPP
LEARNING
MEDIA

Chapter 1 – Introduction to management accounting

Task 1.1

	Financial accounting	Management accounting
Users	External to the organisation	Internal management
Timing	Annual	When required
Type of information	Historic	Historic and future
Format	Specified by law	To be useful

Task 1.2

Cost card	£
Direct Materials	X
Direct labour	X
Direct expenses	X
Prime cost	X
Production overheads	X
Production cost	X
Non-production overheads	
– selling and distribution	X
– administration	X
– finance	X
Total cost	X

Task 1.3

The correct answer is: Planning, control and decision-making only

Management information is used for planning, control and decision making.

Task 1.4

The correct answer is: The total of direct costs

Prime cost is the total of direct material, direct labour and direct expenses.

All costs incurred in manufacturing a product describes total production cost, including absorbed production overhead. **The material cost of a product** is only a part of prime cost.

Task 1.5

Cost card – toy soldier	£
Direct materials Wood and paint	3.50
Direct labour Toy maker's wages	3.00
Direct expenses Hire of special tools	0.50
Prime cost	7.00
Rent, rates, heat and light	0.30
Production cost	7.30
Non-production overheads:	
Advertising and sales promotion	0.70
Total cost	8.00

Task 1.6

Description	Principle
Complying with relevant laws and regulations	Professional behaviour
Not disclosing information to third parties without authority	Confidentiality
Being straightforward and honest in all professional and business relationships	Integrity
Not allowing bias or conflict of interest	Objectivity
Maintaining professional knowledge and skill	Professional competence and due care

Task 1.7

The correct answer is: The costs relating to a component of the business which generates revenue.

Task 1.8

The correct answer is:

	True ✓	False ✓
A budget is used as part of an organisation's planning process	✓	
A budget can be used for cost control	✓	

Chapter 2 – Cost classification and cost behaviour

Task 2.1

Cost types	
Production cost	Factory heat and light
	Depreciation of plant and machinery
Selling and distribution cost	Sales Director's salary
	Depreciation of delivery vans
	Fuel and oil for delivery vans
Administration cost	Finance Director's salary

Task 2.2

The correct answer is: A maintenance assistant in a factory maintenance department.

The maintenance assistant is not working directly on the organisation's output but is performing an indirect task. All the other three options describe tasks that involve working directly on the output.

Task 2.3

The correct answer is: Staples to fix the fabric to the seat of a chair

Indirect costs are those which **cannot be easily identified** with a specific cost unit. Although the staples could probably be identified with a specific chair, the cost is likely to be relatively insignificant. The expense of tracing such costs does not usually justify the possible benefits from calculating more accurate direct costs. The cost of the staples would therefore be treated as an indirect cost, to be included as a part of the overhead absorption rate.

The other options all represent significant costs which can be traced to a specific cost unit. Therefore they are classified as direct costs.

Task 2.4

The correct answer is: A selling and distribution overhead. The deliveries occur after a sale is made, therefore drivers' wages are a selling and distribution overhead.

Task 2.5

Carbon for racquet heads	Direct material
Office stationery	Administration costs
Wages of employees stringing racquets	Direct labour
Supervisors' salaries	Indirect labour
Advertising stand at badminton tournaments	Selling and distribution costs

Task 2.6

Graph A – variable cost per unit

Graph B – total fixed cost across level of activity

Task 2.7

	Output (units)	Total cost £
Highest	26,500	410,000
Lowest	16,000	252,500
Increase	10,500	157,500

Variable cost per unit = 157,500/10,500 = £15 per unit

Fixed cost

16,000 × £15	= £240,000
£252,500 – £240,000	= £12,500

OR

26,500 × £15	= £397,500
£410,000 – £397,500	= £12,500

Task 2.8

The correct answer is Graph 2. Graph 2 shows that costs increase in line with activity levels.

Task 2.9

The correct answer is Graph 1. Graph 1 shows that fixed costs remain the same whatever the level of activity.

BPP
LEARNING
MEDIA

Task 2.10

The correct answer is Graph 1. Graph 1 shows that cost per unit remains the same at different levels of activity.

Task 2.11

The correct answer is Graph 4. Graph 4 shows that semi-variable costs have a fixed element and a variable element.

Task 2.12

The correct answer is Graph 3. Graph 3 shows that the step fixed costs go up in 'steps' as the level of activity increases.

Task 2.13

The correct answer is: £5,100

	Units	£
High output	1,100	18,300
Low output	700	13,500
Variable cost	400	4,800

Variable cost per unit £4,800/400 = £12 per unit

Fixed costs = £18,300 – (£12 × 1,100) = £5,100

Therefore the correct answer is £5,100.

£13,500 is the total cost for an activity of 700 units

£13,200 is the total variable cost for 1,100 units (1,100 × £12)

£4,800 is the difference between the costs incurred at the two activity levels recorded

Task 2.14

The correct answer is variable. In the long run, all costs are variable.

Task 2.15

The correct answer is: £ 76,000

	£
Variable costs 8,000 × £8	64,000
Fixed costs	12,000
	76,000

BPP LEARNING MEDIA

Chapter 3 – Materials and labour costs

Task 3.1

(a) The EOQ is 600 kg = $\sqrt{\dfrac{[2 \times 90{,}000 \times 2]}{1}}$

(b) and (c) Inventory record card – FIFO

Date	Receipts			Issues			Balance	
	Quantity kg	Cost per kg £	Total cost £	Quantity kg	Cost per kg £	Total cost £	Quantity kg	Total cost £
Balance as at 22 September							150	180
24 September	600	1.398	839				750	1,019
26 September				400	1.325	530	350	489
28 September	600	1.402	841				950	1,330
30 September				500	1.398	699	450	631

Note that the cost of the 400 kg issued on 26 September is made up of

      150 kg @ £1.20   = £180

      250 kg @ £1.398 = £350

Total 400 kg   = £530   So the cost per kg = £530 ÷ 400 kg = 1.325

Note that the cost of the 500 kg issued on 30 September is made up of

      350 kg @ £1.398 = £489

      150 kg @ £1.402 = £210

Total 500 kg   = £699   So the cost per kg = £699 ÷ 500 kg = 1.398

ANSWERS

Task 3.2

Inventory record card

Date	Receipts Quantity kg	Receipts Cost per kg £	Receipts Total cost £	Issues Quantity kg	Issues Cost per kg £	Issues Total cost £	Balance Quantity kg	Balance Total cost £
Balance as at 1 January							4,000	10,000
31 January	1,000	2.0	2,000				5,000	12,000
15 February				3,000	2.5	7,500	2,000	4,500
28 February	1,500	2.5	3,750				3,500	8,250
14 March				500	2.5	1,250	3,000	7,000

Task 3.3

Inventory record card – AVCO

Date	Purchases Quantity kg	Purchases Cost £	Purchases Total cost £	Requisitions Quantity kg	Requisitions Cost £	Requisitions Total cost £	Balance Quantity kg	Balance Total cost £
1 Jan							300	7,500
2 Jan				250	25.00	6,250	50	1,250
12 Jan	400	25.75	10,300				450	11,550
21 Jan				200	25.67	5,134	250	6,416
29 Jan				75	25.67	1,925	175	4,491

BPP LEARNING MEDIA

Task 3.4

Date	Receipts			Issues			Balance	
	Quantity kg	Cost per kg £	Total cost £	Quantity kg	Cost per kg £	Total cost £	Quantity kg	Total cost £
1 January	4,000	2.50	10,000				4,000	10,000
31 January	1,000	2.00	2,000				5,000	12,000
15 February				3,000	2.50	7,500	2,000	4,500
28 February	1,500	2.50	3,750				3,500	8,250
14 March				500	2.50	1,250	3,000	7,000

Task 3.5

	Cost £
AVCO issue	£19,890
FIFO issue	£16,205
AVCO balance	£33,462
FIFO balance	£37,147

Workings

AVCO cost per unit = (£15,960 + £23,520 + £13,872)/(840 + 960 + 480) = £53,352/2,280) = £23.40

AVCO issue cost of 850 units = £23.40 × 850 = £19,890

FIFO issue cost of 850 units = 840 units at £19 and 10 units at £24.50 = £15,960 + (10 units × £24.50) = £16,205

AVCO closing balance = (840 + 960 + 480 – 850) × £23.40 = £33,462

FIFO closing balance = ((960 – 10) × £24.50) + £13,872 = £37,147

Task 3.6

The economic order quantity is [300] units.

The formula for the economic order quantity (EOQ) is

$$EOQ = \sqrt{\frac{2cd}{h}}$$

With

c   = £10

ANSWERS

d   = 5,400

h   = £0.10 × 12 months = £1.20

$$EOQ = \sqrt{\frac{2 \times £10 \times 5,400}{£1.20}}$$

$$= \sqrt{90,000}$$

= 300 units

Task 3.7

The economic order quantity is [175] units (to the nearest whole unit).

$$EOQ = \sqrt{\frac{2cd}{h}}$$

$$= \sqrt{\frac{2 \times £100 \times 1,225}{£8}}$$

$$= \sqrt{30,625}$$

= 175 units

Task 3.8

Reorder level = (Average usage × Average lead time) + Inventory buffer

= (100 units × 23 days) + 1,080

= [3,380 units]

Minimum inventory reorder quantity = Average usage per day × Average lead time

= (100 units × 23 days)

= [2,300 units]

Maximum inventory reorder quantity= Maximum inventory level − inventory buffer

= 5,100 units − 1,080 parts

= [4,020 units]

Task 3.9

Cost per EU £ [8]

Closing WIP £ [3,360]

Total production cost = £40,000 + £30,000 + £10,000 = £80,000.

WIP equivalent units = 600 units × 70% = 420 units

Cost per equivalent unit = £80,000 / (9,580 + 420) = £8

The closing WIP value = 420 × £8 = £3,360

BPP
LEARNING
MEDIA

Task 3.10

The correct answer is: Debit: Production overhead control account, Credit: Inventory account

The cost of indirect materials issued is credited to the inventory account and 'collected' in the production overhead control account pending its absorption into production.

Debit Production account and Credit Inventory account represents the entries for the issue to production of **direct materials**.

Debit Cost of sales and Credit Inventory account is not correct. The issue of materials should not be charged direct to cost of sales. The cost of materials issued should first be analysed as direct or indirect and charged to production or the overhead control account accordingly.

Task 3.11

Complete the cost journal entries to record the four payroll payments made last week.

Date	Code	Debit £	Credit £
8 June	DI01 Box manufacture direct costs	5,700	
8 June	WA01 Wages control account		5,700
10 June	DI02 Box painting direct costs	2,350	
10 June	WA01 Wages control account		2,350
12 June	OH01 Operating overheads	1,610	
12 June	WA01 Wages control account		1,610
14 June	OH02 Non-operating overheads	4,080	
14 June	WA01 Wages control account		4,080

Task 3.12

Production account

		£			£
31 May	Wages control	275,000			

Production overhead control

		£			£
31 May	Wages control	75,000			

Task 3.13

The correct answer is: Maintenance workers in a shoe factory. Maintenance workers will not be involved in actually making the shoes. Machinists in a clothes manufacturer will be involved in making the clothes and are therefore direct labour. Bricklayers actually make the buildings so are also direct labour.

Task 3.14

DEBIT Wages control	CREDIT Overhead control		
DEBIT Admin overhead control	CREDIT Wages control		
DEBIT Overhead control	CREDIT Wages control	✓
DEBIT Wages control	CREDIT Admin overhead control		

Indirect wages are 'collected' in the overhead control account, for subsequent absorption into work in progress.

Task 3.15

	Code	Dr £	Cr £
Manufacturing department A wages	2300	18,500	
Manufacturing department A wages	6000		18,500
Manufacturing department B wages	2400	22,500	
Manufacturing department B wages	6000		22,500
Maintenance department wages	3400	12,700	
Maintenance department wages	6000		12,700
General admin department salaries	3500	7,600	
General admin department salaries	6000		7,600

Task 3.16

DEBIT Wages control	CREDIT Production account		
DEBIT Production	CREDIT Wages control account	✓
DEBIT Costs of sales account	CREDIT Production account		
DEBIT Finished goods account	CREDIT Production account		

The **direct costs of production**, of which direct wages are a part, are **debited to the production account**. The credit entry is made in the **wages control account**, where the wages cost has been 'collected' **prior to its analysis** between direct and indirect wages.

Task 3.17

(a) Employee's weekly timesheet for week ending 7 December

	Hours	Total pay £
Basic pay (including basic hours for overtime)	48	720.00
Mon–Fri overtime premium	7	52.50
Sat–Sun overtime premium	6	90.00
Total		862.50

(b) £ | 135

£15 × 30% = £4.50 per unit

30 extra units × £4.50 = £135

(c) 4,200 | units

7,000 units × 60% = 4,200 units

Task 3.18

£ | 0.325

$$\frac{£13,650}{42,000} = £0.325$$

Task 3.19

(a)

Labour cost	Hours	Workings	£
Basic pay	800	800 × £22.00	17,600
Overtime rate 1	50	50 × £33.00	1,650
Overtime rate 2	40	40 × £44.00	1,760
Total cost before bonus	890	890	21,010
Bonus payment		(600 × £8.80)	5,280
Total cost including bonus			26,290

(b) The total labour cost of producing each unit in the month of April is:

> £ | 8.80

£26,290/2,987.50 = £8.80

(c) The basic pay and overtime for each member of department B for April was:

> £ | 5,252.50   and the bonus payable to each team member was:

> £ | 1,320

£21,010/4 = £5,252.50

£5,280/4 = £1,320

BPP LEARNING MEDIA

Chapter 4 – Allocation and apportionment

Task 4.1

	Basis of apportionment	Silicon moulding £	Silicon extrusion £	Maintenance £	Stores £	General Admin £	Totals £
Depreciation of plant and equipment	NBV of plant and equipment	904,669	1,105,706				2,010,375
Power for production machinery	Production machinery power usage (KwH)	572,500	1,215,000				1,787,500
Rent and rates	Floor space			74,648	93,310	93,310	261,268
Light and heat	Floor space			16,500	20,625	20,625	57,750
Indirect labour	Allocated			253,750	90,125	600,251	944,126
Totals		1,477,169	2,320,706	344,898	204,060	714,186	5,061,019
Reapportion Maintenance		120,714	224,184	(344,898)			
Reapportion Stores		81,624	122,436		(204,060)		
Reapportion General Admin		357,093	357,093			(714,186)	
Total overheads to production centres		2,036,600	3,024,419				5,061,019

BPP
LEARNING
MEDIA

Task 4.2

(a)

	Basis of apportionment	Silicon moulding £	Silicon extrusion £	Maintenance £	Stores £	General Admin £	Total £
Depreciation of plant and equipment	Headcount	972,762	1,037,613				2,010,3
Power for production machinery	Headcount	864,919	922,581				1,787,5
Rent and rates	Floor space			74,648	93,310	93,310	261,2
Light and heat	Floor space			16,500	20,625	20,625	57,7
Indirect labour	Allocated			253,750	90,125	600,251	944,1
Totals		1,837,681	1,960,194	344,898	204,060	714,176	5,061,0
Reapportion Maintenance		120,714	224,184	(344,898)			
Reapportion Stores		81,624	122,436		(204,060)		
Reapportion General Admin		464,221	249,965			(714,186)	
Total overheads to production centres		2,504,240	2,556,779				5,061,0

(b) The manager would most likely argue with the revised basis of allocation as his/her costs have increased by £467,640. The use of headcount to apportion machinery costs is not common and the manager could argue that depreciation based on NBV, and power on consumption are better bases for reapportioning these costs. Nonetheless, if the cost centre is using more general admin then it is fair that it should bear more of that cost.

Task 4.3

£	16.50

The full absorption cost of a unit of Em excludes the fixed administration, selling and distribution costs.

£18.20 – £1.70 = £16.50

Task 4.4

Reapportionment – inter-service centre work is ignored here.

Direct method

	Production		Service centres		
	X £	y £	Stores £	Maintenance £	General administration overheads £
Overheads	80,000	50,000	40,000	30,000	8,000
Reapportion Stores (55% and 45%)	22,000	18,000	(40,000)		
Reapportion Maintenance (8,000/ 15,000) and (7,000/ 15,000)	16,000	14,000		(30,000)	
Reapportion General admin overheads (50:50)	4,000	4,000			(8,000)
Total	122,000	86,000			

Task 4.5

Step-down method – inter-service work is taken into account in the first step only.

	Production		Service centres	
	X £	y £	Stores £	Maintenance £
Allocated overhead	80,000	50,000	40,000	30,000
Apportion stores (50:30:20)	20,000	12,000	(40,000)	8,000
				38,000
Apportion maintenance (30:50)	14,250	23,750		(38,000)
Total	114,250	85,750		

BPP
LEARNING
MEDIA

Chapter 5 – Absorption costing

Task 5.1

(a)

	Silicon moulding	Silicon extrusion
Actual direct labour hours	21,222	17,144
Actual machine hours	8,459	6,501
Budgeted overhead absorbed – labour hrs	424,440	342,880
Budgeted overhead absorbed – machine hrs	465,245	357,555

(b)

	Silicon moulding	Silicon extrusion
Actual overheads (£)	425,799	354,416
Difference – labour hrs	1,359	11,536
Difference – machine hrs	39,446	3,139

Task 5.2

The correct answer is: Absorbed overheads exceed actual overheads.

Absorbed overheads exceeding budgeted overheads could lead to under-absorbed overheads if actual overheads far exceeded both budgeted overheads and the overhead absorbed. Actual overheads exceeding budgeted overheads could lead to under-absorbed overheads if overhead absorbed does not increase in line with actual overhead incurred.

Task 5.3

The correct answer is: £405,000

Budgeted absorption rate for fixed overhead	= £360,000/8,000
	= £45 per hour
Fixed overhead absorbed	= 9,000 hours × £45
	= £405,000

If you selected £384,000 you based your absorption calculations on sales units instead of labour hours.

If you selected £432,000 you calculated the correct figure for fixed overhead absorbed but also added the variable overheads.

£459,000 is the figure for actual total overhead incurred.

BPP LEARNING MEDIA

Task 5.4

The correct answer is: under-absorbed by £27,000

Actual fixed overhead incurred	= £432,000
Fixed overhead absorbed	= £405,000 (from Task 6.3)
Fixed overhead under absorbed	= £27,000

If you selected under-absorbed by £72,000, you simply calculated the difference between the budgeted and actual fixed overhead. If you selected under-absorbed by £75,000, you based your absorption calculations on sales units instead of production units. If you selected over-absorbed by £27,000 you performed the calculations correctly but misinterpreted the result as an over absorption.

Task 5.5

Term	Description
Activity based costing	Identifying activities which cause costs to charge overheads to products
Cost driver	A factor influencing the level of cost
Cost pool	Equivalent to a cost centre in traditional absorption costing

Assigning only variable costs to cost units – refers to marginal costing

A cost which cannot be traced directly to a product – refers to an overhead

A unit of product for which costs can be ascertained – refers to a cost unit

Charging whole cost items direct to a cost unit – refers to allocation

Task 5.6

(a)   The correct answer is: Silicon moulding £51/hour, Silicon extrusion £56/hour

(b)   The correct answer is: Silicon moulding £18/hour, Silicon extrusion £17/hour

Task 5.7

	Silicon moulding	Silicon extrusion
Budgeted overheads (£)	450,000	352,520
Budgeted direct labour hours	22,500	17,626
Budgeted machine hours	8,182	6,409

Workings

£450,000/£20 = 22,500 labour hours
£352,520/£20 = 17,626 labour hours
£450,000/£55 = 8,182 machine hours
£352,520/£55 = 6,409 machine hours

Task 5.8

Production overheads absorbed into production	Debit: Production	Credit: Production overheads
Indirect labour transferred to production overheads	Debit: Production overheads	Credit: Wages
Direct materials issued to production	Debit: Production	Credit: Inventory

---

Task 5.9

	Drag and drop choice
Transaction 1	Debit: production overheads, Credit: statement of profit or loss
Transaction 2	Debit: statement of profit or loss, Credit: production overheads

---

Task 5.10

	Debit £	Credit £	No entry in this a/c £
Overhead control account		✓	
Work in progress account			✓
Statement of profit or loss	✓		

Under-absorbed overhead means that the overhead charged to production was too low and so there must be a debit to the statement of profit or loss.

Chapter 6 – Job, batch and service costing

Task 6.1

Service	Cost unit
Road, rail and air transport services	Passenger/kilometre, tonne/kilometre
Hotels	Occupied bed-night
Education	Full-time student
Hospitals	Patient-day
Catering establishments	Meal served

Task 6.2

Job number 03456

	Budget £	Actual £	Variance F/A £
Direct materials			
Plasterboard	3,600.00	3,500.00	100F
Wood & door frames	4,750.00	4,802.00	52A
Insulation	1,050.00	1,145.00	95A
Electrical fittings	320.00	300.00	20F
Windows	2,220.00	2,576.00	356A
Paint	270.00	250.00	20F
Direct labour			
Construction	554.00	641.00	87A
Electrical	224.00	160.00	64F
Decorating	165.00	205.00	40A
Direct expenses			
Hire of specialist lathe	240.00	240.00	0
Overheads (based upon direct labour hours)			
84/90 hours @ £15.00	1,260.00	1,350.00	90A

Task 6.3

(a) and (b)

	Budget £	Actual £	Variance F/A £	%
Direct materials				
Plasterboard	3,600.00	3,500.00	100F	2.8
Wood & door frames	4,750.00	4,802.00	52A	1.1
Insulation	1,050.00	1,145.00	95A	9.0
Electrical fittings	320.00	300.00	20F	6.3
Windows	2,220.00	2,576.00	356A	16.0
Paint	270.00	250.00	20F	7.4
Direct labour				
Construction	554.00	641.00	87A	15.7
Electrical	224.00	160.00	64F	28.6
Decorating	165.00	205.00	40A	24.2
Direct expenses				
Hire of specialist lathe	240.00	240.00	0	0
Overheads (based upon direct labour hours)				
84/90 hours @ £15.00	1,260.00	1,350.00	90A	7.1
Total cost	14,653.00	15,169.00	516.00 A	
Profit	2,930.60	2,414.60		
Net price	17,583.60	17,583.60		
VAT at 20%	3,516.72	3,516.72		
Total price	21,100.32	21,100.32		

(c)   (2,930.60 – 2,414.60)/2,930.60 = 17.6%

Task 6.4

	✓
High levels of indirect costs as a proportion of total cost	✓
Cost units are often intangible	✓
Use of composite cost units	✓
Use of equivalent units	

In service costing it is difficult to identify many attributable direct costs. Many costs must be treated as indirect costs and shared over several cost units, therefore there are high levels of indirect costs as a proportion of total cost. Many services are intangible, for example a haircut or a cleaning service provide no physical, tangible product. Composite cost units such as passenger-mile or bed-night are often used in service costing. 'Use of equivalent units' does not apply because equivalent units are more often used in costing for tangible products.

Task 6.5

(a) £ | 18.20

$$\frac{582,400}{32,000} = £18.20$$

(b) £ | 16.50

$$\frac{582,400 - 54,400}{32,000} = £16.50$$

(c) £ | 528,000

£16.50 × 32,000 units = £528,000 or £582,400 − £54,400

= £528,000

ANSWERS

Chapter 7 – Standard costing and budgeting

Task 7.1

	True ✓	False ✓
A standard cost is a planned unit cost	✓	
Standard costing can be used to value inventory	✓	

Task 7.2

	Working	Standard cost £
Material A	7kg × £1	7
Material B	4 litres × £2	8
Material C	3 metres × £3	9
Total		24

Task 7.3

	True ✓	False ✓
Standard material cost per unit = standard material usage x standard material cost per unit of material	✓	
Standard costing can be used as a control device	✓	
Standard costing provides actual future costs		✓
Standard costing provides information for budgeting	✓	

Task 7.4

	✓
0.80 litres	
1.00 litres	
1.20 litres	
1.25 litres	✓

1 litre × (100/80) = 1.25 litres

Task 7.5

The standard labour cost of a product can be established by multiplying the...	Gap 1	by the...	Gap 2

Gap 1	✓
price per litre	
price per kg	
rate per hour	✓

Gap 2	✓
number of labour hours per unit	✓
Total number of units	

Task 7.6

Batches produced and sold	3,000 £	3,750 £	5,000 £
Sales revenue	60,000	75,000	100,000
Variable costs:			
Direct materials 1.90	5,700	7,125	9,500
Direct labour 9	27,000	33,750	45,000
Overheads 3.1	9,300	11,625	15,500
Semi-variable costs:	9,450		
Variable element		7,500	10,000
Fixed element		3,450	3,450
Total cost	51,450	63,450	83,450
Total profit	8,550	11,550	16,550
Profit per batch (to 2 decimal places)	2.85	3.08	3.31

Workings

Sales revenue   £60,000/3,000 batches = £20 per batch
Direct materials   £5,700/3,000 batches = £1.90 per batch
Direct labour   £27,000/3,000 batches = £9 per batch
Variable overheads   £9,300/3,000 batches = £3.1 per batch

(Note that the overheads are variable and therefore we calculate a cost per batch. If they were fixed overheads then the cost would be the same for 3,000 batches, 3,750 batches and 5,000 batches.)

Semi-variable cost   7,500   £18,450
                                          7,000   £9,450
                                            500   9,000

Variable cost = £9,000/500 = £2 per batch

Fixed cost = £18,450 – (7,500 × £2) = £3,450

Task 7.7

Batches produced and sold	3,000 £	3,750 £	5,000 £
Sales revenue	60,000	75,000	100,000
Variable costs:			
Direct materials 2	6,000	7,500	10,000
Direct labour 10	30,000	37,500	50,000
Overheads 3.2	9,600	12,000	16,000
Semi-variable costs:	9,450		
Variable element		7,500	10,000
Fixed element		3,450	3,450
Total cost	55,050	67,950	89,450
Total profit	4,950	7,050	10,550
Profit per batch (to 2 decimal places)	1.65	1.88	2.11

Task 7.8

Batches produced and sold	3,000 £	4,000 £
Sales revenue	60,000	80,000
Variable costs:		
Direct materials	6,000	8,000
Direct labour	30,000	40,000
Overheads	9,600	12,800
Semi-variable costs:		
Variable element	6,000	8,000
Fixed element	3,450	3,450
Total cost	55,050	72,250
Total profit	4,950	7,750
Profit per batch (to 2 decimal places)	1.65	1.94

Reject.

The profit per batch is less than £2 at 4,000 batches, so management should reject the order.

Task 7.9

Batches produced and sold	3,000 £	5,000 £	7,000 £
Sales revenue	90,000	150,000	210,000
Variable costs:			
Direct materials	13,500	22,500	31,500
Direct labour	31,500	52,500	73,500
Overheads	18,000	30,000	42,000
Semi-variable costs:	9,450		
Variable element		10,000	14,000
Fixed element		3,450	3,450
Total cost	72,450	118,450	164,450
Total profit	17,550	31,550	45,550
Profit per batch (to 2 decimal places)	5.85	6.31	6.51

Task 7.10

Batches produced and sold	4,000 £	6,000 £	9,000 £
Sales revenue	140,000	210,000	315,000
Variable costs:			
Direct materials	22,000	33,000	49,500
Direct labour	50,000	75,000	112,500
Overheads	28,000	42,000	63,000
Semi-variable costs:	16,750	22,750	31,750
Total cost	116,750	172,750	256,750
Total profit	23,250	37,250	58,250
Profit per batch (to 2 decimal places)	5.81	6.21	6.47

Task 7.11

	True ✓	False ✓
A fixed budget can never be changed		✓
A rolling budget is continually updated	✓	
A rolling budget allows a more accurate budget to be produced	✓	

BPP LEARNING MEDIA

Chapter 8 – Variance analysis

Task 8.1

	Flexed Budget	Actual	Variance	Favourable F or Adverse A
Volume sold	156,000	156,000		
	£000	£000	£000	
Sales revenue	1,248	1,326	78	F
Less costs:				
Direct materials	390	372	18	F
Direct labour	468	444	24	F
Overheads	225	250	25	A
Operating profit	165	260	95	F

Task 8.2

	Flexed Budget	Actual	Budget unit cost/revenue	Actual unit cost/revenue
Volume sold	156,000	156,000		
	£000	£000		
Sales revenue	1,248	1,326	8	8.50
Less costs:				
Direct materials	390	372	2.50	2.38
Direct labour	468	444	3	2.85
Overheads	225	250		
Operating profit	165	260	1.06	1.67

They are all true. The unit selling price is higher than budgeted, which may be due to a rise in the sales price not planned for in the budget, or fewer bulk discounts to customers if these were planned for. The lower unit price for materials may arise from bulk buying discounts or new cheaper sources of supply. The lower labour costs may be due to a change in the make up of employees so there are more lower paid employees, or efficiency savings so fewer employees make the same number of units.

Task 8.3

	Original budget	Flexed budget	Actual	Variance
Number of packets	40,000	32,000	32,000	
	£	£	£	£
Sales revenue	130,000	104,000	96,000	−8,000
Less costs:				
Direct materials and direct labour	48,000	38,400	36,800	1,600
Variable overheads	22,000	17,600	19,200	−1,600
Fixed overheads	14,200	14,200	13,600	600
Profit from operations	45,800	33,800	26,400	

Task 8.4

	Original budget	Flexed budget	Actual	Variance
Number of books	60,000	45,000	45,000	
	£	£	£	£
Sales revenue	1,140,000	855,000	910,200	55,200
Less costs:				
Direct materials and direct labour	480,000	360,000	375,000	−15,000
Variable overheads	540,000	405,000	406,400	−1,400
Fixed overheads	56,000	56,000	55,000	1,000
Profit from operations	64,000	34,000	73,800	

BPP LEARNING MEDIA

Task 8.5

(a)

	Original budget	Flexed budget	Actual	Variance
Number of cans	30,000	25,000	25,000	
	£	£	£	£
Sales revenue	22,500	18,750	18,000	−750
Less costs:				
Direct materials and direct labour	10,500	8,750	8,500	250
Variable overheads	6,000	5,000	4,200	800
Fixed overheads	4,000	4,000	4,100	−100
Profit from operations	2,000	1,000	1,200	

(b) Referring to your answer for part (a), which one of the variances has had the greatest impact in increasing the profit from operations?

	✓
Sales revenue	
Direct materials and direct labour	
Variable overheads	✓
Fixed overheads	

(c) Which one of the following might have caused the variance for direct materials and direct labour costs?

	✓
A decrease in material prices	✓
An increase in employees' pay	
An increase in material prices	
Less efficient usage of direct labour	

Chapter 9 – Marginal costing

Task 9.1

(a)   Absorption costing – unit cost

	£
Direct materials	8.50
Direct labour	17.00
Variable overheads	3.00
Prime cost	28.50
Fixed overheads ((£850,000/250,000) × 2)	6.80
Absorption cost	35.30

(b)   Marginal costing – unit cost

	£
Direct materials	8.50
Direct labour	17.00
Variable overheads	3.00
Prime cost or marginal cost	28.50

Task 9.2

In the long run, total profit for a company will be | the same for both types of costing | whether marginal costing or absorption costing is used.

Task 9.3

It might be argued that | absorption costing | is preferable to | marginal costing | **in management accounting,** in order to be consistent with the requirement of current accounting standards and financial reporting.

BPP
LEARNING
MEDIA

Task 9.4

(a) £ | 45,400

		£	£
Sales	(5,200 × £30)		156,000
Direct materials	(5,800 × £6)	34,800	
Direct labour	(5,800 × £7.50)	43,500	
Variable overhead	(5,800 × £2.50)	14,500	
		92,800	
Less closing inventory	(600 × £16)	9,600	
			(83,200)
Contribution			72,800
Less fixed costs			27,400
			45,400

(b) £ | 48,400

		£	£
Sales	(5,200 × £30)		156,000
Materials	(5,800 × £6)	34,800	
Labour	(5,800 × £7.50)	43,500	
Variable overhead	(5,800 × £2.50)	14,500	
Fixed costs	(5,800 × £5)	29,000	
Less closing inventories	(600 × £21)	(12,600)	
			(109,200)
Over-absorbed overhead (W)			1,600
Absorption costing profit			48,400

Working

		£
Overhead absorbed	(5,800 × £5)	29,000
Overhead incurred		27,400
Over-absorbed overhead		1,600

Task 9.5

(a) | £ | 36.40 |

$$\frac{£582,400}{16,000} = £36.40$$

(b) | £ | 33.00 |

$$\frac{£582,400 - £54,400}{16,000} = £33.00$$

(c) | £ | 528,000 |

£33.00 × 16,000 units = £528,000 (or £582,400 − £54,400 = £528,000)

(d) | £ | 454,400 |

£176,000 + £230,400 + £48,000 = £454,400

(e) | £ | 28.40 |

$$\frac{£454,400}{16,000} = £28.40$$

BPP LEARNING MEDIA

Chapter 10 – Short-term decision-making

Task 10.1

(a) $\boxed{9{,}000 \text{ units}}$ Breakeven point in units = Fixed costs/contribution per unit

$\qquad$ = £45,000/(£22 – £17)

$\qquad$ = 9,000 units

(b) $\boxed{£\ 198{,}000}$ Breakeven point in units × selling price per unit

$\qquad$ = 9,000 × £22

$\qquad$ = £198,000

(c)

Units of COLIN sold	9,500	10,500
	£	£
Margin of safety (units)	500	1,500
Margin of safety percentage	$\left(\dfrac{500}{9{,}500} \times 100\%\right) = 5\%$	$\left(\dfrac{1{,}500}{10{,}500} \times 100\%\right) = 14\%$
Margin of safety revenue (units × sales price)	11,000	33,000

(d) $\boxed{13{,}000 \text{ units}}$ Activity level = $\dfrac{\text{Fixed costs + target profit}}{\text{Contribution per unit}} = \dfrac{45{,}000 + 20{,}000}{5}$

$\qquad$ = 13,000 units

(e) The correct answer is: the breakeven point will decrease and the margin of safety will increase

---

Task 10.2

(a) 8,000 × £(22 – 17) = £40,000

(b) $\boxed{£\ 132{,}000}$ which is (£30,000/£5 × £22) or (6,000 × £22)

(c)

Units of COLIN sold	6,500	7,000
	£	£
Margin of safety (units)	500	1,000
Margin of safety percentage	$\left(\dfrac{500}{6{,}500} \times 100\%\right) = 8\%$	$\left(\dfrac{1{,}000}{7{,}000} \times 100\%\right) = 14\%$

(d) $\boxed{8{,}000 \text{ units}}$ Yes as it is at the maximum level of production.

BPP
LEARNING
MEDIA

Task 10.3

The correct answer is 3,000 units

$$\text{Breakeven point} = \frac{\text{Fixed costs}}{\text{Contribution per unit}} = \frac{£30,000}{£(15-5)} = 3,000 \text{ units}$$

If you selected 2,000 units you divided the fixed cost by the selling price, but remember that the selling price also has to cover the variable cost. 4,000 units is the margin of safety, and if you selected 6,000 units, you divided the fixed cost by the variable cost per unit.

Task 10.4

The correct answer is: 20%

$$\text{Breakeven point} = \frac{\text{Fixed costs}}{\text{Contribution per unit}} = \frac{£96,000}{£(12-8)} = 24,000 \text{ units}$$

Budgeted sales   30,000 units

Margin of safety   6,000 units

$$\text{Expressed as a \% of budget} = \frac{6,000}{30,000} \times 100\% = 20\%$$

If you selected 25% you calculated the correct margin of safety in units, but you then expressed this as a percentage of the breakeven point. If you selected 73% you divided the fixed cost by the selling price to determine the breakeven point, but the selling price also has to cover the variable cost. You should have been able to eliminate 125% as an option; the margin of safety expressed as a percentage must always be less than 100 per cent.

Task 10.5

(a)   The correct answer is: 10,090 units

$$\text{Breakeven point} = \frac{\text{Fixed costs}}{\text{Contribution per unit}}$$

$$= \frac{10,000 \times £(4.00 + 0.80)}{(£6.00 - (£1.20 + £0.40))}$$

$$= \frac{£48,000}{£4.40} = 10,909 \text{ units}$$

If you selected 8,000 units you divided the fixed cost by the selling price, but the selling price also has to cover the variable cost. 8,333 units ignores the selling costs, but these are costs that must be covered before the breakeven point is reached. 10,000 units is the budgeted sales volume, which happens to be below the breakeven point.

(b)   The correct answer is: 13,409 units

Contribution required for target profit = fixed costs + profit

                                                              = £48,000 + £11,000

                                                              = £59,000

÷ Contribution per unit (from part (a)) = £4.40

∴ Sales units required   = 13,409 units

If you selected 2,500 units you divided the required profit by the contribution per unit, but the fixed costs must be covered before any profit can be earned. If you selected 9,833 units you identified correctly the contribution required for the target profit, but you then divided by the selling price per unit instead of the contribution per unit. 10,625 units ignores the selling costs, which must be covered before a profit can be earned.

Task 10.6

(a)

Forecast	Top4	Top5	Total
Contribution per unit (£) (W1)	6	9	
Contribution per kg (£) (W2)	16	18	
Ranking	2	1	
Total material available (kg)			1,125
Material allocated (kg)	375	750	
Number of units produced (W3)	1,000	1,500	
Total contribution earned (£) (W4)	6,000	13,500	19,500
Less: fixed costs (£)			10,000
Forecast profit/loss made (£)			9,500

Workings

W1:   Top4 – £18,000/3,000 = £6

　　　Top5 – £13,500/1,500 = £9

W2:   Top4 – £18,000/1,125 = £16

　　　Top5 – £13,500/750 = £18

W3:   Top4 kg per unit = 1,125 kg/3,000 = 0.375 kg

　　　∴ 375 kg/0.375 kg per unit = 1,000 units

W4:   Top4 = 1,000 units × £6 = £6,000

　　　Top5 = 1,500 units × £9 = £13,500

(b)   Contract Top5 | should | be selected as the first contract to produce next month as it has the highest | contribution per kg used | .

Task 10.7

Forecast	Sun	Rain	Total
Contribution per unit (£) (W1)	3	4	
Contribution per hour (£) (W2)	4	2	
Ranking	1	2	
Total labour hours available (hours)			5,000
Labour hours allocated (hours)	2,250	2,750	
Number of units produced (W3)	3,000	1,375	
Total contribution earned (£) (W4)	9,000	5,500	14,500
Less: fixed costs (£)			7,000
Forecast profit/loss made (£)			7,500

Workings

W1: Sun – £9,000/3,000 = £3

Rain – £6,000/1,500 = £4

W2: Sun – £9,000/2,250 = £4

Rain – £6,000/3,000 = £2

W3: Rain hours per unit = 3,000/1,500 = 2 hours

∴ 2,750 hours/2 hours per unit = 1,375 units

W4: Sun = 3,000 units × £3 = £9,000

Rain = 1,375 units × £4 = £5,500

BPP
LEARNING
MEDIA

Chapter 11 – Cash management

Task 11.1

The working capital operating cycle is the...	Gap 1	Liquid assets include...	Gap 2

Gap 1	✓
period between cash being paid for purchases and cash received for sales	
inventory holding period plus trade receivables' collection period less trade payables' payment period	✓

Gap 2	✓
Non-current assets	
Cash, receivables and inventory	✓

Task 11.2

The correct answer is: 4 months

	Months
Raw material inventory holding period	4.0
Less: credit taken from suppliers	(3.0)
Finished goods inventory holding period	1.0
Trade receivables' collection period	2.0
Working capital cycle	4.0

Task 11.3

The correct answer is: 51 days

Working:

	Days
Inventory holding period	51
Trade receivables' collection period	77
	128
Less: trade payables' payment period	(41)
Working capital cycle	87

Task 11.4

The correct answer is: Offering an early settlement discount to customers

Offering an early settlement discount to customers will hopefully encourage customers to pay earlier. This will have the effect of reducing the trade receivables' collection period, which will in turn reduce the working capital cycle of the business.

Task 11.5

The correct answer is: £39,500

The carrying amount of non-current assets increased by £27,000 but this was after deducting £12,500 of depreciation, so the cash paid for new assets must have been £27,000 + £12,500 = £39,500.

Task 11.6

The correct answer is: £1,960 loss

The carrying amount of the machine at the date of disposal is £25,760 (64,400 – 38,640). If it is sold for £23,800, it must have been sold at a loss of £1,960 (23,800 – 25,760).

Task 11.7

Which of the following statements about working capital (WC) is correct?

	✓
WC is the difference between a company's total assets and its total liabilities	
WC is the difference between a company's total assets and its current liabilities	
WC is the difference between a company's current assets and its total liabilities	
WC is the difference between a company's current assets and its current liabilities	✓

Task 11.8

Which of the following is not classed as working capital?

	✓
Overdraft	
Inventory	
Accruals	
Bank loan	✓

A bank loan is not working capital because it is not a current liability.

Task 11.9

(a) Purchases budget

	April kgs	May kgs	June kgs	July kgs
Materials required for production				
April 1,220 × 2 kg	2,440			
May 1,320 × 2 kg		2,640		
June 1,520 × 2 kg			3,040	
July 1,620 × 2 kg				3,240
Opening inventory	– 550	– 500	– 450	– 400
Closing inventory	500	450	400	350
Purchases in kgs	2,390	2,590	2,990	3,190

Cost of material purchases	April £	May £	June £	July £
April 2,390 × £40	95,600			
May 2,590 × £40		103,600		
June 2,990 × £40			119,600	
July 3,190 × £40				127,600

(b) Cash payments to suppliers for May to July

	May £	June £	July £
Cash payments	95,600	103,600	119,600

Task 11.10

Labour budget – hours	April Hours	May Hours	June Hours
April 7,050/3	2,350		
May 6,450/3		2,150	
June 6,000/3			2,000
Cash payment for wages – £	**April £**	**May £**	**June £**
April 2,350 × £8.40	19,740		
May 2,150 × £8.40		18,060	
June 2,000 × £8.40			16,800

ANSWERS

Chapter 12 – Spreadsheets

Task 12.1

- Open the renamed spreadsheet and open the subs worksheet.

    - Format the data on this page as a table, include the headings.

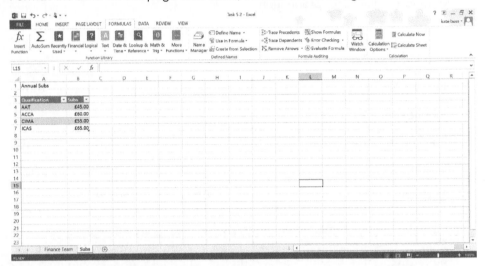

    - On the finance team worksheet, use a VLOOKUP function to complete the subs column.

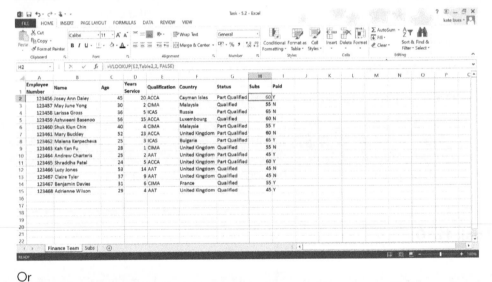

Or

    - Format the subs figures in a red font colour.

BPP
LEARNING
MEDIA

- Use conditional formatting to highlight all employees aged 40 and over.

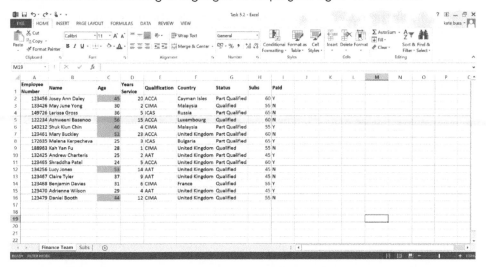

- Sort the data based on employee number, from lowest to highest.

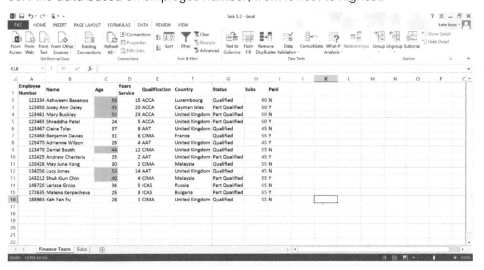

- Rename Column J as 'holiday'.

  - Use an IF statement to complete the data in this column to show how many days holiday per year to which each individual is entitled.

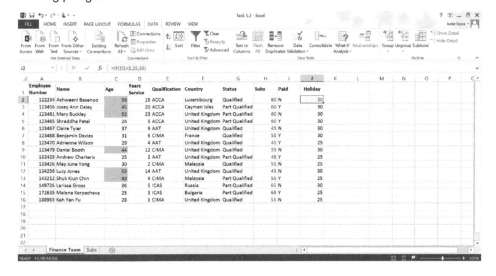

- Format the data as a table with light blue shading.
  - Use the filter function to display only individuals who are members or students of the AAT who have not yet paid their subs.

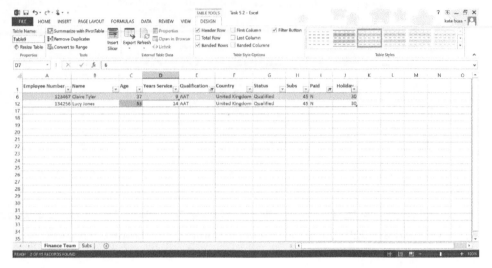

Task 12.2

- Open the renamed spreadsheet.
  - Use find and replace to update any cells which refer to 'Cater co' to show the name of the new company.

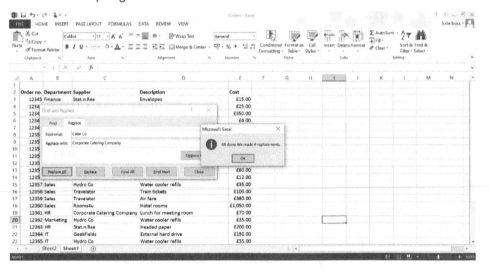

  - Rename the worksheet 'order list'.

- Create a pivot table and pivot chart in a new worksheet to represent the amount spent with each supplier.

    - Rename the chart as 'Spend per supplier'.

    - Rename the worksheet 'Supplier spend' and ensure the order of the worksheets is such that the order list worksheet is on the left and the supplier spend worksheet is on the right.

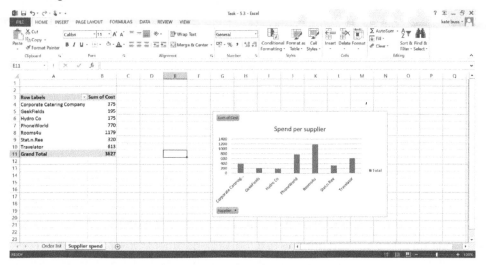

- Return to the Order List worksheet and format the data as a table using data style medium 14.

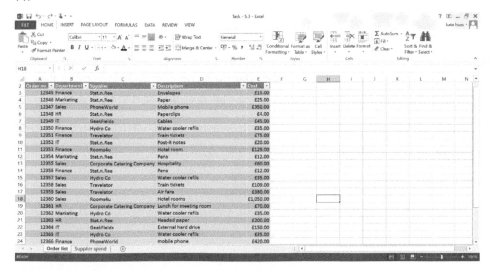

- Protect the workbook so that no changes can be made to the source data and the hidden sheets remain hidden (greyed out if attempt to unhide).

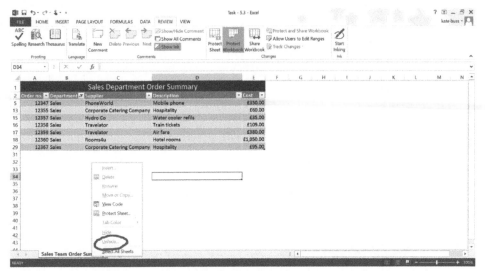

- Use the SaveAs feature to save a copy of this version of the spreadsheet called 'Sales Team Order Summary'.

Task 12.3

- Open the renamed spreadsheet.
  - Add a formula to cell C31 to calculate the amount of flexi-time earned or used on Monday. Apply this formula to the rest of the days of the week.

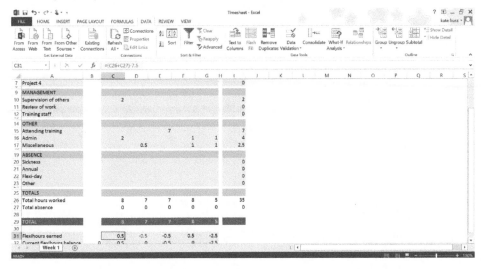

BPP
LEARNING
MEDIA

- Add a formula to cell C32 to calculate the current balance of flexitime on Monday. Apply this formula to the rest of the days of the week.

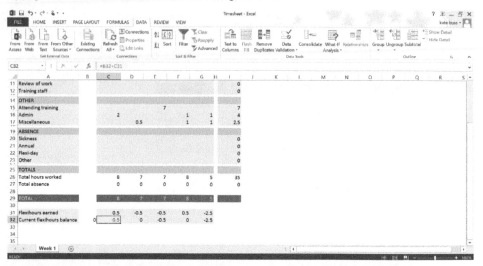

- Replace the formulas in cells I25 and I28 with more robust formulas to check for errors in the summing of data.

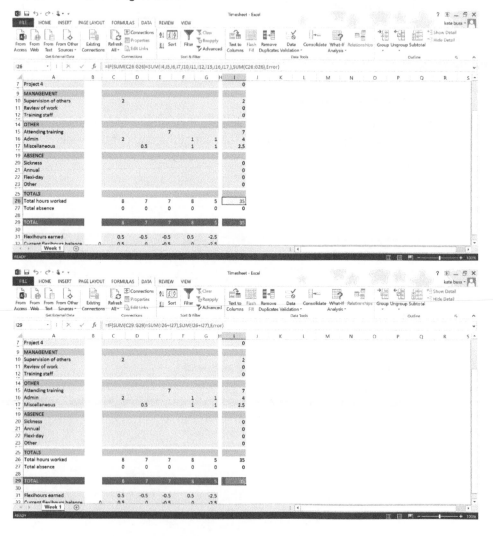

BPP LEARNING MEDIA

- Use a data validation function in cells C28:G28 to identify any days where less than six hours are worked.

  - Set the data validation to circle in red any days where fewer than six hours have been worked.

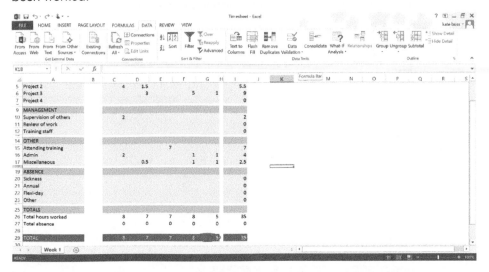

- Use a data validation function to prevent more than two hours of admin being charged on any given day.

  - Attempt to change the admin charge on Monday to three hours.

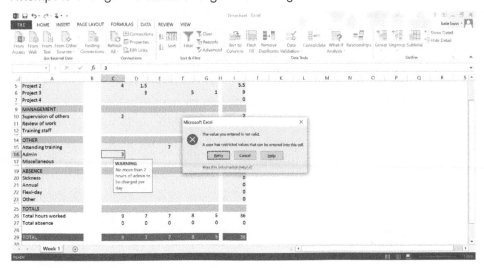

- Insert two new worksheets.

  - Change the name of the new worksheets to 'Week 2' and 'Week 3'

  - Copy the format and formulas used on Week 1 to Week 2 and Week 3 and populate the spreadsheets with the information given above.

  - Link the formula related to flexi-time to ensure the balance from week 1 is carried over to Week 2 and so on.

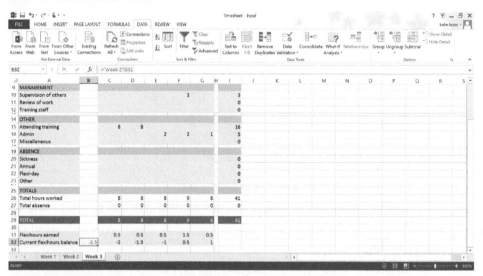

- Insert a new worksheet and rename it 'Summary'.

  - Use the data from Weeks 1–3 to produce a summary sheet which collates the total number of hours charged to each activity per week.

  - Format the summary sheet in the same style as the weekly worksheets.

  - Use the split function to keep the header rows in place.

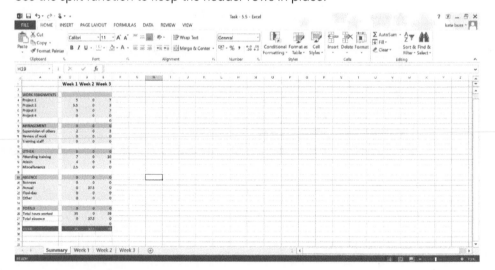

Task 12.4

- Open the renamed spreadsheet and go into the Record tab.

  - Use a lookup function to complete the employee name column.

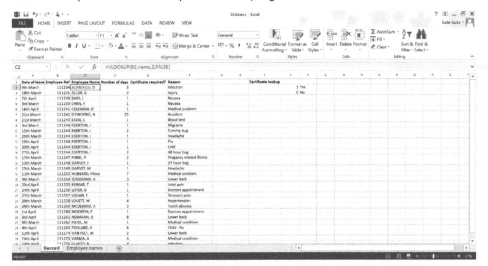

- Use an IF statement in Column I along with a lookup function in Column E to determine whether or not a certificate is required.

  - The IF statement should return the values 0 for no and 1 for yes and the lookup should refer to the table in Columns J and K.

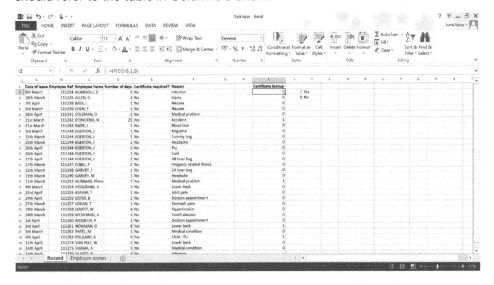

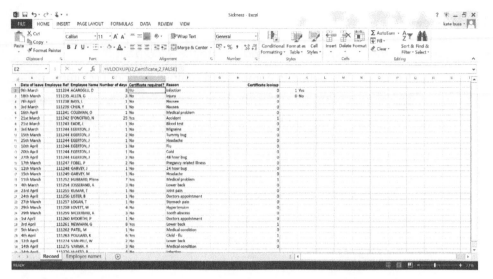

– Hide Columns I, J and K.

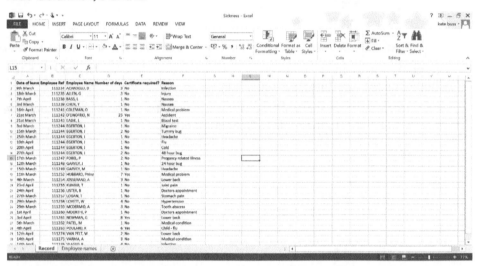

- Insert a pivot table on a new worksheet which summarises the total number of sickness days taken by each employee.

  – Rename this worksheet 'Summary'.

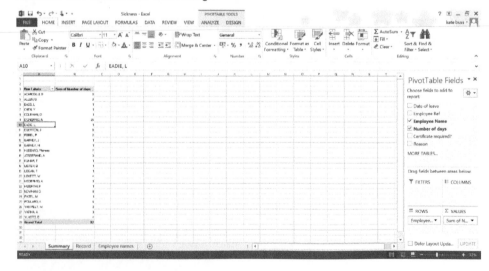

BPP LEARNING MEDIA

- Return to the 'Record' worksheet and sort the data by employee number.

    - Use a subtotal function to count the instances of sickness taken by each individual.

    - Highlight the entire worksheet and apply conditional formatting to highlight the employee number of any individuals who are at risk of falling into the frequent sickness category.

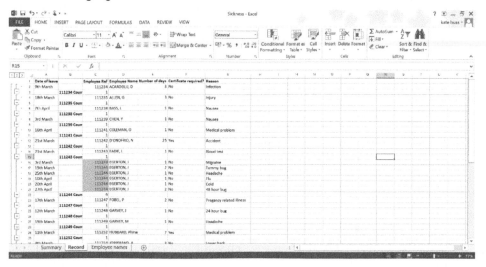

Task 12.5

- Open the renamed spreadsheet.

    - Run a data validation test to remove any duplicate entries.

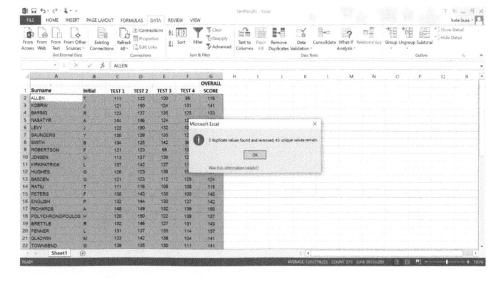

BPP
LEARNING
MEDIA

- Select the entire worksheet, copy the contents and paste this into a new worksheet.

  - Rename the new worksheet 'Sales team order summary'.

  - Apply filters to the data to show only data relating to orders raised by the sales team.

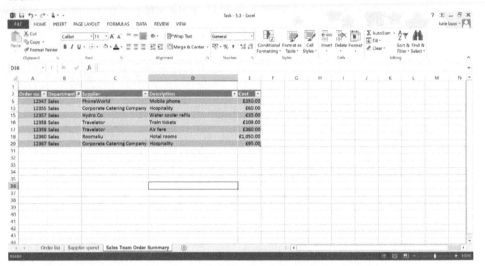

- Merge cells A1:E1 and add the text 'Sales Department Order Summary'.

  - Change the font size in the merged cell to 16 and centre the text.

  - Use the fill function to make the merged cell dark green and change the font colour in this cell to white.

  - Remove the gridlines.

- Prepare the document for being sent to the sales team. It is important that the sales team can see only their worksheet and none of the workings or data for the other departments.

  - Hide the worksheets 'Order list' and 'Supplier Spend'.

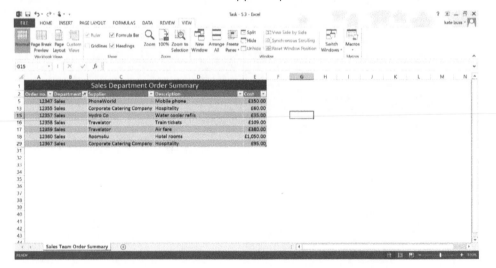

BPP LEARNING MEDIA

- Prepare a histogram based on the overall scores achieved by the students.
  - The bins used should be in intervals of 10, beginning with 100.
  - Change the axis to 'No. students' and 'total score'.
  - Change the title of the histogram to 'Overall score analysis'.

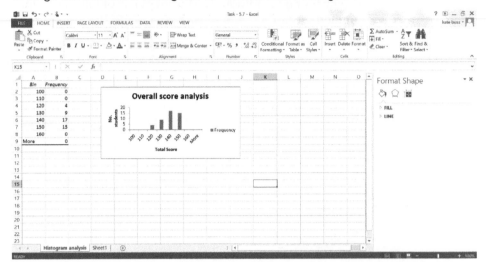

- Return to worksheet 'test results' and format the data as a table using table style medium 12.
  - Use the filters within the table to identify only those students who will be offered an interview for the scholarship program.

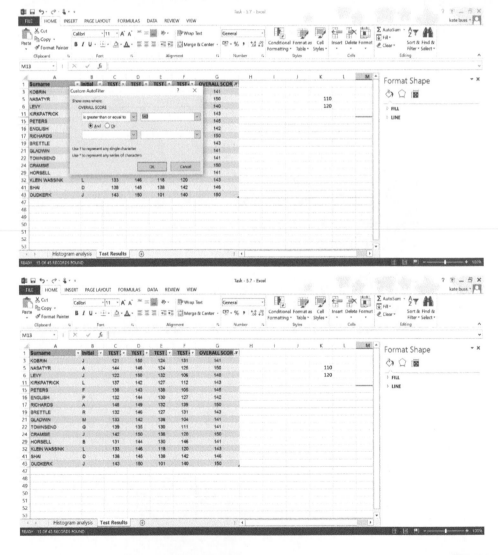

– Reorder the data using the filter to rank the potential scholarship candidates from highest scoring to lowest scoring.

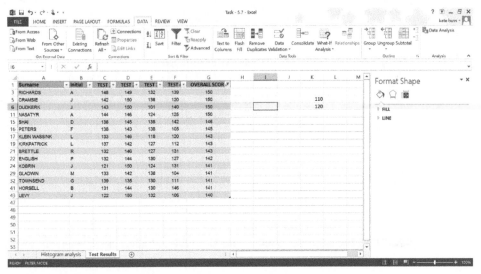

- Add a column called 'outcome' in Column H

  – Insert the text 'Scholarship' in this column next to the top 5 students, and Interview against the remaining students.

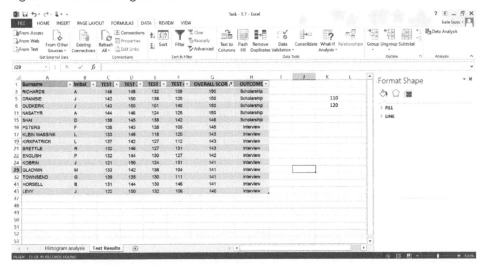

  – Remove the filters, and then refilter to show only students who are below average.

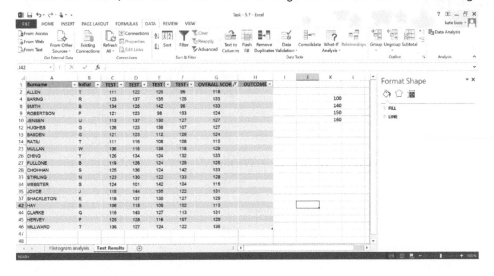

BPP
LEARNING
MEDIA

- Add the text Refer in the outcome box for these students.

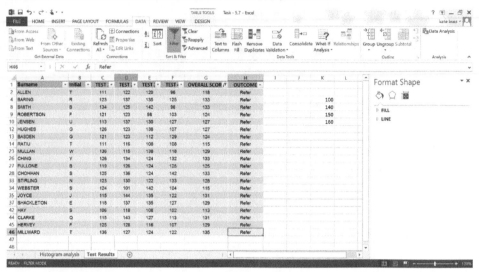

- Remove the filters.

- Filter using the outcome filter to identify all students who have passed the tests but who are not contenders for the scholarship program.

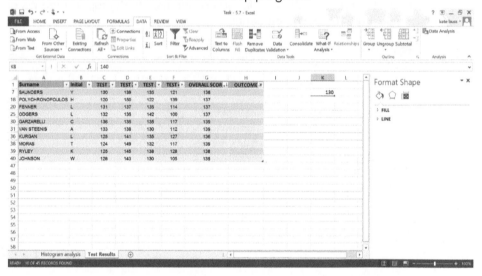

Task 12.6

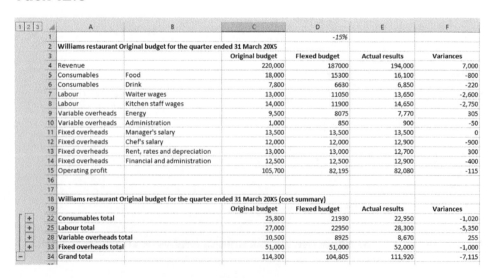

	A	B	C	D	E	F
1			-15%			
2	Williams restaurant Original budget for the quarter ended 31 March 20X5					
3			Original budget	Flexed budget	Actual results	Variances
4	Revenue		220,000	187000	194,000	7,000
5	Consumables	Food	18,000	15300	16,100	-800
6	Consumables	Drink	7,800	6630	6,850	-220
7	Labour	Waiter wages	13,000	11050	13,650	-2,600
8	Labour	Kitchen staff wages	14,000	11900	14,650	-2,750
9	Variable overheads	Energy	9,500	8075	7,770	305
10	Variable overheads	Administration	1,000	850	900	-50
11	Fixed overheads	Manager's salary	13,500	13,500	13,500	0
12	Fixed overheads	Chef's salary	12,000	12,000	12,900	-900
13	Fixed overheads	Rent, rates and depreciation	13,000	13,000	12,700	300
14	Fixed overheads	Financial and administration	12,500	12,500	12,900	-400
15	Operating profit		105,700	82,195	82,080	-115
16						
17						
18	Williams restaurant Original budget for the quarter ended 31 March 20X5 (cost summary)					
19			Original budget	Flexed budget	Actual results	Variances
22	Consumables total		25,800	21930	22,950	-1,020
25	Labour total		27,000	22950	28,300	-5,350
28	Variable overheads total		10,500	8925	8,670	255
33	Fixed overheads total		51,000	51,000	52,000	-1,000
34	Grand total		114,300	104,805	111,920	-7,115

BPP LEARNING MEDIA

Task 12.7

	A	B	C	D	E	F	G
1				15%			
2	Westside Hospital Original budget for the year ended 31 May 20X6						
3		Budget item	Original budget	Flexed budget	Actual results	Variances	Adverse/Favourable
4							
5		Income	3,420,000	3,933,000	3,933,000	0	
6	Variable costs	Catering	440,000	506,000	511,000	5,000	A
7	Variable costs	Laundry	120,000	138,000	142,000	4,000	A
8	Variable costs	Pharmacy	560,000	644,000	638,000	6,000	F
9	Staff costs	Supervisors	150,000	150,000	160,000	10,000	A
10	Staff costs	Nurses	184,000	230,000	244,000	14,000	A
11	Staff costs	Assistants	352,000	416,000	421,000	5,000	A
12	Fixed costs	Administration	750,000	750,000	790,000	40,000	A
13	Fixed costs	Security	80,000	80,000	82,000	2,000	A
14	Fixed costs	Rent and property	780,000	780,000	800,000	20,000	A
15	Surplus/(Deficit)		4,000	239,000	145,000	94,000	A

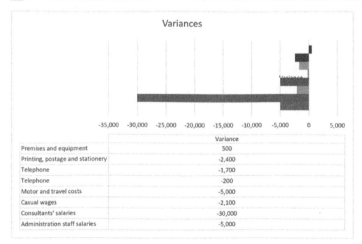

Task 12.8

	A	B	C	D	E	F	G
1					110%		
2	Farrell Co Original budget for the year ended 30 June 20X7						
3			Master budget	Actual results	Flexed budget	Variance	Variance
4			£	£	£	£	%
5	Revenue		2,000,000	2,100,000	2,200,000	-100,000	-4.5%
6	Fixed overheads	Administration staff salaries	100,000	105,000	100,000	-5,000	-5.0%
7	Fixed overheads	Consultants' salaries	960,000	990,000	960,000	-30,000	-3.1%
8	Variable overheads	Casual wages	14,000	17,500	15,400	-2,100	-13.6%
9	Fixed overheads	Motor and travel costs	75,000	80,000	75,000	-5,000	-6.7%
10	Fixed overheads	Telephone	8,000	8,200	8,000	-200	-2.5%
11	Variable overheads	Telephone	18,000	21,500	19,800	-1,700	-8.6%
12	Variable overheads	Printing, postage and stationery	16,000	20,000	17,600	-2,400	-13.6%
13	Fixed overheads	Premises and equipment	24,000	23,500	24,000	500	2.1%
14	Operating profit		785,000	834,300	980,200	-145,900	-14.9%

Variances

	Variance
Premises and equipment	500
Printing, postage and stationery	-2,400
Telephone	-1,700
Telephone	-200
Motor and travel costs	-5,000
Casual wages	-2,100
Consultants' salaries	-30,000
Administration staff salaries	-5,000

To add a data table, click on the graph and select the add button on the right hand side to display 'chart elements', then click on 'data table'.

Task 12.9

C21 | =SUMIF($A$5:$A$14,$A21,C$5:C$14)

			Flexed		
		Original	budget	Actual	Variances
	A	B	C	D	E	F
3			budget	11,500	results	11,500
4						
5	Revenue		600,000	690,000	700,000	10,000
6	Materials	A	40,000	46,000	49,000	-3,000
7	Materials	B	44,000	50,600	56,000	-5,400
8	Materials	C	32,000	36,800	39,200	-2,400
9	Direct labour	Skilled	72,000	82,800	87,000	-4,200
10	Direct labour	Unskilled	36,000	41,400	44,000	-2,600
11	Variable overheads	Supervision	42,000	48,300	51,000	-2,700
12	Variable overheads	Production planning	22,000	25,300	26,700	-1,400
13	Fixed overheads	Sales and distribution	25,000	25,000	26,500	-1,500
14	Fixed overheads	Finance and administration	22,000	22,000	22,700	-700
15	Operating profit		265,000	311,800	297,900	-13,900
16						
17						9
18						
19	Carter Co Overhead summary for the quarter ended 30 June 20X8					
				Flexed		
			Original	budget	Actual	Variances
20			budget	11,500	results	11,500
21	Materials		116,000	133,400	144,200	-10,800
22	Direct labour		108,000	124,200	131,000	-6,800
23	Variable overheads		64,000	73,600	77,700	-4,100
24	Fixed overheads		47,000	47,000	49,200	-2,200
25	Total costs		335,000	378,200	402,100	-23,900

Task 12.10

	A	B	C
1		Breakeven calculations	
2	Revenue	1,500,000	
3	Variable costs		
4	Direct materials	500,000	
5	Direct labour	350,000	
6	Assembly	80,000	
7	Packaging	70,000	
8	Total variable costs	1,000,000	
9	Variable costs per unit	40	
10	Contribution per unit	20	
11	Fixed costs		
12	Assembly	120,000	
13	Packaging	210,000	
14	Total fixed costs	330,000	
15	Breakeven point in units	16,500	
16	Breakeven point in revenue	990,000	
17	Contribution/Sales ratio	0.33	
18	Margin of safety in units	8,500	
19	Margin of safety in %	34.00	HIGHER
20	Target profit volume	25,500	LESS

BPP LEARNING MEDIA

AAT Q2022 Assessment

Management Accounting Techniques

Students should attempt the AAT practice assessments on the AAT's Lifelong Learning portal prior to taking the actual assessment.

BPP
LEARNING
MEDIA

BPP Practice Assessment 1

Management Accounting Techniques

Time allowed: 2 hours 30 minutes

BPP
LEARNING
MEDIA

Management Accounting Techniques (MATS)
BPP practice assessment 1

Task 1 (24 marks)

This task is about costing techniques.

(a)   (i)   Identify whether the following statements are true or false.

Statement	True ✓	False ✓
Batch costing is a system that is used in business that provides individual, 'one-off' products for customers.		
Service costing often involves the use of composite cost units.		
Job costing keeps a separate record of costs incurred on each job.		

(3 marks)

(ii)   Identify which TWO of the following would use job costing.

	✓
Hospital	
Electrician	
Car manufacturer	
Plumber	

(3 marks)

A business issues indirect materials to production from inventory.

(iii)   Identify the journal entries required to record this transaction.

Account	DR ✓	CR ✓
Production		
Direct costs		
Production overhead		
Inventory		

(2 marks)

The Metal extrusion department of Claridges Ltd uses batch costing for some of its products.

The product DD1 is made in one batch of 62,000 units and the budgeted costs are as follows.

Description	Cost per batch £
Direct material	77,500
Direct labour	83,700
Variable overheads	12,400
Fixed manufacturing overheads	31,000
Fixed administration, selling and distribution costs	18,600
Total costs	223,200

(b) (i) Calculate the total cost of one unit of DD1.

The total cost of one unit of DD1 is £ ☐

(2 marks)

(ii) Calculate the full absorption cost of one unit of DD1.

The full absorption cost of one unit of DD1 is £ ☐

(2 marks)

(iii) Calculate the marginal cost of one unit of DD1.

The marginal cost of one unit of DD1 is £ ☐

(2 marks)

(iv) Calculate the marginal production cost of one batch of DD1.

The marginal production cost of one batch of DD1 is £ ☐

(2 marks)

(v) Calculate the full absorption cost of one batch of DD1.

The full absorption cost of one batch of DD1 is £ ☐

(2 marks)

(c) (i) Which of the following means the total direct costs?

	✓
Production cost	
Variable cost	
Overhead cost	
Prime cost	

(2 marks)

(ii) Which of the following principles means being straightforward and honest?

	✓
Objectivity	
Integrity	
Confidentiality	
Competence	

(2 marks)

(iii) Which of the following shows how particular sections of the business generate sales, costs and profits?

	✓
Segmented report	
Financial report	
Overhead report	
Inventory report	

(2 marks)

Task 2 (24 marks)

This task is about attributing costs.

Claridges Ltd apportions overheads using the most appropriate basis.

(a)   (i)   Complete the table below to identify a suitable basis for allocating or apportioning each overhead by selecting the most appropriate option from the picklist.

Overhead	Basis of apportionment	
Depreciation of equipment		▼
Power for production machinery		▼
Rent and rates for admin department		▼
Equipment insurance		▼
Canteen costs		▼

Picklist:

Factory floor space
Head office floor space
NBV of equipment
Number of employees
Number of orders executed
Number of production runs
Production machinery power usage (KwH)

(4 marks)

(ii)   Claridges Ltd has already allocated and apportioned its current overhead costs for the next period as shown in the table below. These costs have yet to be apportioned to the two departments of Glass moulding and Glass extrusion.

- 45% of the Maintenance cost centre's time is spent maintaining production machinery in the Glass moulding production centre, and the remainder in the Glass extrusion production centre.

- The Stores cost centre makes 35% of its issues to the Glass moulding production centre, and 65% to the Glass extrusion production centre.

- General Administration supports the two production centres equally.

- There is no reciprocal servicing between the three support cost centres.

Complete the table showing the reapportionment of overheads to the two production centres. Enter your answers in whole pounds only. Use minus signs or brackets to indicate any negative figures.

	Basis of apportionment	Glass moulding £	Glass extrusion £	Maintenance £	Stores £	General Admin £	Totals £
Depreciation of plant and equipment	NBV of plant and equipment	312,708	437,792				750,500
Power for production machinery	Production machinery power usage (KwH)	1,028,963	846,037				1,875,000
Rent and rates	Floor space			40,167	48,200	32,133	120,500

	Basis of apportionment	Glass moulding £	Glass extrusion £	Maintenance £	Stores £	General Admin £	Totals £
Light and heat	Floor space			10,833	13,000	8,667	32,500
Indirect labour	Allocated			115,000	37,850	225,000	377,850
Totals		1,341,671	1,283,829	166,000	99,050	265,800	3,156,350
Reapportion Maintenance							
Reapportion Stores							

	Basis of apportionment	Glass moulding £	Glass extrusion £	Maintenance £	Stores £	General Admin £	Totals £
Reapportion General Admin							
Total overheads to production centres							

(12 marks)

Claridges Ltd has the following information about two of its departments:

Quarter 1	Metal bashing	Metal extrusion
Budgeted direct labour hours	42,750	24,750
Budgeted machine hours	13,145	8,250
Actual direct labour hours	43,100	22,275
Actual machine hours	12,936	8,975
Budgeted overheads	£814,990	£445,500
Actual overheads	£789,765	£495,250

(b)   (i)   Calculate the budgeted overhead absorption rate for the Metal bashing department based on machine hours, and that for the Metal extrusion department based on direct labour hours. Show your answers to TWO decimal places.

	Metal bashing £	Metal extrusion £
Budgeted overhead absorption rate	☐ per hour	☐ per hour

(4 marks)

Now suppose for Quarter 2 that the overhead absorption rate for the Metal extrusion department had been based on direct machine hours, and was £55 per hour. The actual overheads were £462,500 and the actual machine hours were 8,500 hours.

(ii) Complete the following table.

	Overheads incurred £	Overheads absorbed £	Difference absorbed £	Under/over absorption £
Metal extrusion profit centre				▼

Picklist:

over
under

(2 marks)

(iii) Refer to the information for Quarter 1, at the start of part (b) of the task, and complete the following sentence.

In Quarter 1 overheads for the Metal bashing department were

▼ by £ [   ] .

Picklist:

over-absorbed
under-absorbed

(2 marks)

Task 3 (24 marks)

This task is about short-term decision making.

The following eight options are costs incurred by Claridges Ltd during the quarter.

(a)   (i)   Select the correct cost behaviour option for each cost.

	Fixed cost	Variable cost	Semi-variable cost	Stepped cost
Material cost of £3 per unit				
Rent cost of £300				
Labour cost of £10 per unit				
Telephone bill of £20 per quarter plus £0.50 per phone call				
Supervisor cost of £5,000				
Insurance cost of £150				
Machine leasing cost £500 per 4,000 units				
Machinery depreciation of £100 based on machine hours used				

(8 marks)

(ii)   Another overhead is estimated to be £570,000 for the period. It consists of a fixed element and a variable element. The fixed element is 30% of the total cost and the rest is variable. The fixed element of the total cost is to be apportioned between the glass moulding and glass intrusion centres in the ratio 65:35. The variable element of the total cost is apportioned in the ratio 46:54.

Complete the following sentences by inserting the correct values.

The fixed element that will be apportioned to the glass extrusion profit centre is:

£ [   ]

The variable element that will be apportioned to the glass moulding profit centre is:

£ [   ]

(4 marks)

(iii)   Identify whether the following statements are true or false.

Statement	True ✓	False ✓
As activity levels increase, the total semi-variable cost decreases.		
As activity levels increase, the semi-variable cost **per unit** decreases.		

(2 marks)

BPP
LEARNING
MEDIA

(b) (i) Choose the correct description for each of the two terms below.

Term	Description
Breakeven point	▼
Target profit	▼

Picklist:

(Contribution per unit x target activity level) less fixed costs
Excess of actual sales over breakeven sales
Excess of breakeven sales over actual sales
Planned revenue less costs
Point where selling price equals variable costs
Profit level before fixed costs
Sales revenue where there is neither profit nor loss
Sales volume where there is neither profit nor loss
Selling price less variable costs
Selling price plus variable costs

(2 marks)

Claridges Ltd manufactures the alphapop, which has a selling price of £20 per unit, and a total variable cost of £12 per unit. Claridges Ltd estimates that the fixed costs per quarter associated with this product are £46,000.

(ii) Calculate the budgeted breakeven, in units, for the alphapop.

[   ] units

(2 marks)

(iii) Calculate the budgeted breakeven, in £s, for the alphapop.

£ [   ]

(2 marks)

(iv) Calculate the margin of safety (in units) if Claridges sells 6,000 units of alphapop.

[   ] units

(2 marks)

(v) If Claridges Ltd wishes to make a profit of £20,000, how many units of the alphapop must it sell?

[   ] units

(2 marks)

Task 4 (16 marks)

This task is about understanding principles of budgeting and of cash management.

(a) (i) Complete the following statement about budgets.

A budget that has been prepared based on actual volumes is called

☐   ... a fixed budget

☐   ... a flexed budget

☐   ... a rolling budget

☐   ... a variable budget

(1 mark)

(ii) Identify whether the following statements are true or false.

	True ✓	False ✓
Standard costs can be used to develop budgets		
A standard labour cost per unit = labour rate per unit x number of hours per unit		

(2 marks)

(iii) Complete the following statement.

A report that allows actual figures to be compared with budget figures and variances to be calculated is called

☐   ... a fixed budget

☐   ... an operating statement

☐   ... an operating budget

(1 mark)

(b) (i) XYZ Ltd currently has a working capital cycle of 35 days. It plans to introduce a new product range which will increase the inventory holding period by 5 days and increase the time taken to collect cash from customers by 14 days.

What is the new working capital cycle? ☐ days.

(2 marks)

(ii) The working capital cycle is the period of time that a business takes to pay its suppliers.

☐   True

☐   False

(1 mark)

(iii) Complete the table by ticking the correct boxes to show whether an item affects cash or profit.

	Cash ✓	Profit ✓
Sales on credit		
Purchase of non-current asset		
Depreciation		
Accrual of expenses		
Receipts from credit customers		

(5 marks)

(c) JEB Ltd is worried that it may go over its overdraft limit because it plans to buy a new non-current asset.

Which THREE of the following are suitable actions to help prevent this?

	✓
Delay payments to suppliers	
Delay capital expenditure	
Increase credit period for customers	
Increase levels of inventory	
Take out a bank loan for capital expenditure	

(4 marks)

BPP LEARNING MEDIA

Task 5 (16 marks)

This task is about the preparation of budgets.

BetterYou is a company which provides short training courses. There are four trainers, Alex, Janine, Simone and Karesh.

BetterYou offers four training packages. Level 1, Level 2 and Level 3. The fourth package 'Complete Mindfulness' incorporates Levels 1–3 and is provided at a reduced cost compared to booking the courses individually.

You have been given a spreadsheet **BetterYou.xls** which shows sales figures achieved by each trainer for the April–June quarter in 20X6. It contains two worksheets: 'Sales' and 'Price structure'.

Download this spreadsheet file from www.bpp.com/aatspreadsheets and save in the appropriate location. Rename it using the following format: **'your initial-surname-AAT no –dd.mm.yy-PA1Task5'.**

For example: J-Donnovan-123456-12.03xx-PA1Task5.

A **high degree of accuracy** is required. You **must save your work as an .XLS or .XLSX file** at regular intervals to avoid losing your work.

(a) Complete the following in the 'Sales' worksheet:

   (i)   Insert a column between the columns 'course' and 'units' and give the column the title 'unit price'. (1 mark)

   (ii) In column D (from cell D2 to cell D49), use a lookup function to insert the unit price on the sales tab, by using the information from the Price structure worksheet. (2 marks)

   (iii) Add a column in Column F called 'Total value' and apply a formula to all cells in that column to show the total value of the units sold in each row. (2 marks)

   (iv) Use the autosum function in cell F50 to determine the total value of sales for the quarter. (1 mark)

   (v)   Format the numbers in this column to contain a thousand separator and make the contents of cell F50 bold. (1 mark)

(b) (i)   On a new worksheet, create a pivot table and pivot chart showing the total value of sales, broken down by course, made by each of Alex, Janine, Simone and Karesh. (4 marks)

   (ii) Rename this sheet 'Total values'. (1 mark)

   (iii) Add a chart title 'Total sales value Apr–Jun'. (1 mark)

(c) (i)   Create a new copy of the sales worksheet and name it 'Budget sales' (1 mark)

         In July to September, total sales are predicted to be 5% less than total sales for April to Jul.

   (ii) In column H, use a formula to calculate the budget sales value for each row and give the column the title 'Budget sales Jul - Sep'. (2 marks)

Task 6 (16 marks)

This task is about budgets and deviations.

Maxwell Co is a company that manufactures high quality cosmetic creams.

The company had originally budgeted to make and sell 40,000 units of cosmetic cream in the quarter to 31 March 20X4. However, it actually made and sold 45,000 units in the quarter.

Information about the original budget and the actual results are provided.

Download the spreadsheet file "PA1 Task 6 - Maxwell Co.xlsx" from www.bpp.com/aatspreadsheets. Save the spreadsheet file in the appropriate location and rename it in the following format: 'your initial-surname-AAT no-dd.mm.yy-PA1Task6'. For example: H-Darch-123456-12.03.xx-PA1Task6

A **high degree of accuracy** is required. You must **save your work** at regular intervals to avoid losing your work.

Complete the following in the Question worksheet.

(a)   (i)   Open this renamed file. Calculate the percentage to flex this budget in line with the information about sales and insert this percentage figure into cell D1. (1 mark)

        (ii)   In cell D3 enter the title Flexed budget. Calculate the flexed budget for cells D5:D14 using absolute referencing where appropriate.   (3 marks)

        (iii)   In cell E3 enter the title Actual results. Use copy and paste to take the actual results from the information you've been given into the correct positions in Column E.   (1 mark)

        (iv)   In cell F3 insert the title Variances. Calculate the variances for each revenue and each cost, showing adverse variances as negative figures with a minus sign. Show these in Column F.   (6 marks)

        (v)   In cell A15 insert the title Operating profit. Use a formula to calculate the operating profit for the original budget, flexed budget and actual results.   (1 mark)

        (vi)   Calculate the overall variance in cell F15.   (1 mark)

        (vii)   Use conditional formatting in Column F to show all favourable variances in green and adverse variances in red.   (2 marks)

        (viii)   Make sure all column headings are in bold.   (1 mark)

BPP Practice Assessment 1 Management Accounting Techniques Answers

Management Accounting Techniques (MATS)
BPP Practice Assessment 1

Task 1

(a) (i)

Statement	True ✓	False ✓
Batch costing is a system that is used in business that provides individual, 'one-off' products for customers.		✓
Service costing often involves the use of composite cost units.	✓	
Job costing keeps a separate record of costs incurred on each job.	✓	

Batch costing is a costing system that gathers together the costs of production of an entire batch of a similar product in order to find the cost of each individual item in that batch.

(ii)

	✓
Hospital	
Electrician	✓
Car manufacturer	
Plumber	✓

A hospital is likely to use service costing and a car manufacturer is likely to use unit costing or batch costing.

(iii) **Identify the journal entries required to record this transaction.**

Account	DR ✓	CR ✓
Production		
Direct costs		
Production overhead	✓	
Inventory		✓

(b) (i)

£	3.60

£223,200/62,000 = £3.60 per unit

(ii)

£	3.60

$$\frac{223,200 - 18,600}{62,000} = £3.30$$

(iii)

£	2.80

$$\frac{77,500 + 83,700 + 12,400}{62,000} = £2.80$$

ANSWERS

(iv) £ | 173,600

£2.80 × 62,000 = £173,600

(v) £ | 204,600

£223,200 − 18,600 = £204,600 (or £3.30 × 62,000 = £204,600)

(c) (i)

	✓
Production cost	
Variable cost	
Overhead cost	
Prime cost	✓

Production cost is the total of the manufacturing costs.

Variable cost are costs which vary directly in line with changes in the level of activity. They can be direct or indirect.

Overhead cost is the sum of the indirect costs.

(ii)

	✓
Objectivity	
Integrity	✓
Confidentiality	
Competence	

Objectivity means not allowing bias, conflict of interest or undue influence of others to override judgements.

Confidentiality means not disclosing information to third parties without authority.

Competence means keeping up to date with professional knowledge and skill.

(iii)

	✓
Segmented report	✓
Financial report	
Overhead report	
Inventory report	

A financial report may not show details for particular sections of the business.

An overhead report will only show overhead details.

An inventory report will only show inventory details.

BPP LEARNING MEDIA

Task 2

(a) (i)

Overhead	Basis of apportionment
Depreciation of equipment	NBV of equipment
Power for production machinery	Production machinery power usage (KwH)
Rent and rates for admin department	Head office floor space
Equipment insurance	NBV of equipment
Canteen costs	Number of employees

(ii)

	Basis of apportionment	Glass moulding £	Glass extrusion £	Maintenance £	Stores £	General Admin £	Totals £
Depreciation of plant and equipment	NBV of plant and equipment	312,708	437,792				750,500
Power for production machinery	Production machinery power usage (KwH)	1,028,963	846,037				1,875,000
Rent and rates	Floor space			40,167	48,200	32,133	120,500
Light and heat	Floor space			10,833	13,000	8,667	32,500
Indirect labour	Allocated			115,000	37,850	225,000	377,850
Totals		1,341,671	1,283,829	166,000	99,050	265,800	3,156,350
Reapportion Maintenance		74,700	91,300	−166,000			
Reapportion Stores		34,668	64,382		−99,050		
Reapportion General Admin		132,900	132,900			−265,800	
Total overheads to production centres		1,583,939	1,572,411				3,156,350

(b) (i)

	Metal bashing £	Metal extrusion £
Budgeted overhead absorption rate	62.00 per hour	18.00 per hour

Workings:

Metal bashing overhead absorption rate = £814,990/13,145 = £62.00

Metal extrusion overhead absorption rate = £445,500/24,750 = £18.00

Now suppose for Quarter 2 that the overhead absorption rate for the Metal extrusion profit centre had been based on direct machine hours, and was £55 per hour. The actual overheads were £462,500 and the actual machine hours were 8,500 hours.

(ii)

	Overheads incurred £	Overheads absorbed £	Difference absorbed £	Under/over absorption
Metal extrusion profit centre	462,500	467,500	5,000	Over

Overheads absorbed = £55 × 8,500 machine hours = £467,500

(iii) In Quarter 1 overheads for the Metal bashing profit centre were

over-absorbed	by	£	12,267

Metal bashing overheads absorbed = £62.00 × 12,936 machine hrs = £802,032

Over-absorption = £802,032 – £789,765 = £12,267

Task 3

(a) (i)

	Fixed cost	Variable cost	Semi-variable cost	Stepped cost
Material cost of £3 per unit		✓		
Rent cost of £300	✓			
Labour cost of £10 per unit		✓		
Telephone bill of £20 per quarter plus £0.50 per phone call			✓	
Supervisor cost of £5,000	✓			
Insurance cost of £150	✓			
Machine leasing cost £500 per 4,000 units				✓
Machinery depreciation of £100 based on machine hours used		✓		

(ii) The fixed element that will be apportioned to the glass extrusion profit centre is:

£	59,850

Fixed element = £570,000 × 30% = £171,000

Fixed element for glass extrusion = £171,000 × (35/100) = £59,850

The variable element that will be apportioned to the glass moulding profit centre is:

£	183,540

Variable element = £570,000 × 70% = £399,000

Variable element for glass moulding = £399,000 × (46/100) = £183,540

(iii)

Statement	True ✓	False ✓
As activity levels increase, the total semi-variable cost decreases.		✓
As activity levels increase, the semi-variable cost **per unit** decreases.	✓	

As activity levels increase, the total semi-variable cost increases. As activity levels increase, the semi-variable cost **per unit** decreases. This is because the cost is made up of a fixed element and a variable element. As the activity level increases the fixed element remains fixed in total, but the fixed cost **per unit** will fall as the total cost is split over more units. The variable element per unit remains the same.

(b)   (i)

Term	Description
Breakeven point	Sales volume where there is neither profit nor loss
Target profit	(Contribution per unit × target activity level) less fixed costs

(ii)   5,750 units

£46,000/£8 = 5,750

(iii)   £ 115,000

5,750 × £20 = £115,000

(iv)   250 units

6,000 − 5,750 = 250 units

(v)   8,250 units

(£20,000/8) + 5,750 = 8,250

Task 4

(a)   (i)   Complete the following statement about budgets.

A budget that has been prepared based on actual volumes is called

☐   ... a fixed budget

✓   ... a flexed budget

☐   ... a rolling budget

☐   ... a variable budget

(ii)

	True ✓	False ✓
Standard costs can be used to develop budgets	✓	
A standard labour cost per unit = labour rate per unit x number of hours per unit		✓

A standard labour cost per unit = labour rate per **hour** x number of hours per unit

(iii) A report that allows actual figures to be compared with budget figures and variances to be calculated is called

☐ ... a fixed budget

✓ ... an operating statement

☐ ... an operating budget

(b) (i) 54 days

(35 + 5 + 14 = 54)

(ii) False

The cash operating cycle is the period of time between cash being paid for raw materials and cash being received from customers for goods sold.

(iii)

	Cash	Profit
Sales on credit		✓
Purchase of non-current asset	✓	
Depreciation		✓
Accrual of expenses		✓
Receipts from credit customers	✓	
Dividend	✓	

(c)

	✓
Delay payments to suppliers	✓
Delay capital expenditure	✓
Increase credit period for customers	
Increase levels of inventory	
Take out a bank loan for capital expenditure	✓

Task 5

(a) (i) Insert a column between the columns 'course' and 'units' and give the column the title 'unit price'.

(ii) Use a lookup function to insert the unit price on the sales tab.

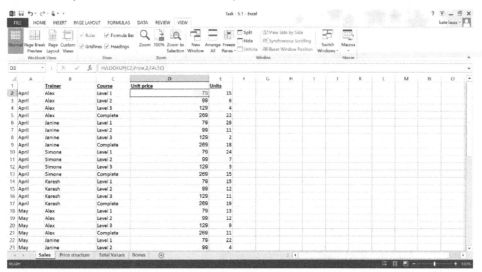

(iii) Add a column in Column F called 'Total value' and apply a formula to all cells in that column to show the total value of the units sold in each row.

(iv) Use the autosum function in cell F50 to determine the total values of sales for the quarter.

(v) Format the numbers in this column to contain a thousand separator and make the contents of cell F50 bold.

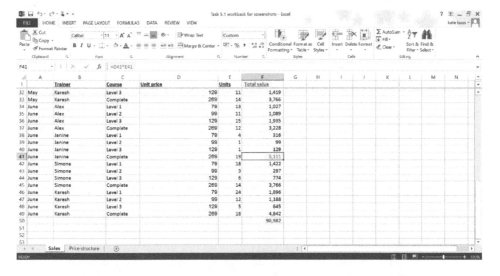

(b) (i) On a new worksheet, create a pivot table and pivot chart showing the total value of sales, broken down by course, made by each of Alex, Janine, Simone and Karesh.

(ii) Rename this sheet 'Total Values'.

(iii) Add a chart title 'Total sales value Apr–Jun'.

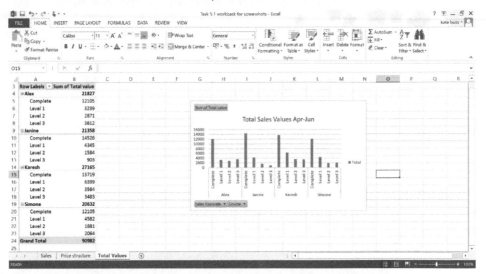

(c) (i) Create a new copy of the sales worksheet and name it 'Budget sales'

In July to September, total sales are predicted to be 5% less than total sales for April to Jul.

(ii) In column H, use a formula to calculate the budget sales value for each row and give the column the title 'Budget sales Jul - Sep'.

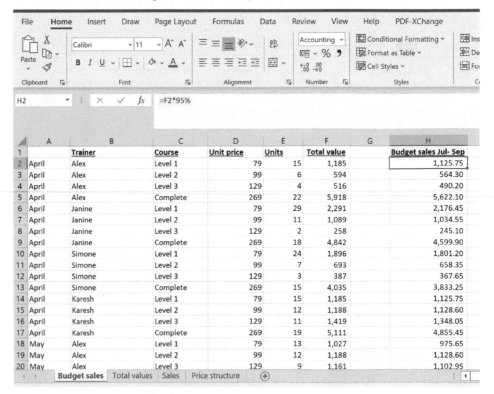

Task 6

	A	B	C	D	E	F
1				112.50%		
2	Maxwell Co Original budget for the quarter ended 31 March 20X4					
3			Original budget	Flexed budget	Actual results	Variances
4						
5	Revenue		920,000	1,035,000	1,040,000	5,000
6	Materials	Silk powder	264,000	297,000	300,000 -	3,000
7	Materials	Silk amino acids	32,000	36,000	37,500 -	1,500
8	Materials	Aloe vera	224,000	252,000	225,000	27,000
9	Direct labour	Skilled	30,000	33,750	37,100 -	3,350
10	Direct labour	Unskilled	15,000	16,875	17,500 -	625
11	Variable overheads	Supervision	30,000	33,750	36,200 -	2,450
12	Variable overheads	Quality control	25,000	28,125	35,100 -	6,975
13	Fixed overheads	Sales and distribution	18,000	18,000	22,400 -	4,400
14	Fixed overheads	Administration	8,000	8,000	7,900	100
15	Operating profit		274,000	311,500	321,300	9,800

ANSWERS

BPP
LEARNING
MEDIA

BPP Practice Assessment 2

Management Accounting Techniques

Time allowed: 2 hours 30 minutes

Management Accounting Techniques (MATS)
BPP Practice Assessment 2

Task 1 (24 marks)

This task is about costing techniques

(a)　(i)　Which of the following describes the control process?

	✓
The action of monitoring something to keep it on course.	
The choice between alternatives.	
The development of strategies to achieve objectives.	
The establishment of a plan for a future period.	

(2 marks)

(ii)　A company carries out production in accordance with the special requirements of each customer.

Which costing method is most appropriate?

	✓
Batch costing	
Job costing	
Unit costing	
Service costing	

(2 marks)

A business finishes the production of a batch of units.

(iii)　Identify the journal entries required to record this transaction.

Account	DR ✓	CR ✓
Finished goods		
Production		

(2 marks)

JEB Ltd is planning to produce a new type of chocolate bar called the Jasper bar. It will be manufactured in batches of 80,000 bars.

The following cost estimates have been produced per batch of Jasper bars.

Jasper bar cost estimates	£
Direct material per batch	2,575
Direct labour per batch	2,625
Variable production overheads per batch	2,100
Fixed production overheads per batch	850
Administration, selling and distribution costs per batch	1,025
Total costs	9,175

(b) (i) Calculate the estimated prime cost per BATCH of Jasper bars.

£ ☐

(2 marks)

(ii) Calculate the estimated marginal production cost per BATCH of Jasper bars.

£ ☐

(2 marks)

(iii) Calculate the estimated full absorption cost of one BATCH of Jasper bars.

£ ☐

(2 marks)

(iv) Calculate the estimated marginal production cost of one Jasper bar (round to TWO decimal places).

£ ☐

(2 marks)

(v) Calculate the estimated full absorption cost of one Jasper bar (round to TWO decimal places).

£ ☐

(2 marks)

(vi) Which of the following describes all variable costs?

	✓
Marginal costs	
Period costs	
Prime costs	
Product costs	

(2 marks)

(c)   (i)   The inventory account for a company for March looks like this:

Inventory account

	£		£
Balance b/d	30,000	Production	100,000
Suppliers	122,500	Overhead control	30,000
Production	45,000	Balance c/d	67,500
	197,500		197,500
Balance b/d	67,500		

Which of the following statements are correct?

(i)   Issues of direct materials during March were £45,000

(ii)   Issues of direct materials during March were £100,000

(iii)   Issues of indirect materials during March were £30,000

(iv)   Purchases of materials during March were £122,500

	✓
(i) and (iv) only	
(ii) and (iv) only	
(ii), (iii) and (iv) only	
All of them	

(2 marks)

(ii)   Which of the following is the correct formula for the economic order quantity?

☐ $EOQ = \sqrt{\dfrac{2cd}{h}}$

☐ $EOQ = \sqrt{\dfrac{2hd}{c}}$

☐ $EOQ = \dfrac{\sqrt{2ch}}{d}$

☐ $EOQ = \dfrac{\sqrt{2c}}{hd}$

Where   h is the cost of holding one unit in inventory for one year

           d is the annual demand

           c is the cost of placing an order   (2 marks)

(iii) The raw materials issued to a job were overestimated and the excess is being sent back to the materials store.

Which document is required?

	✓
Stores credit note	
Stores debit note	
Materials returned note	
Materials transfer note	

(2 marks)

Task 2

A manufacturing organisation has two production departments, A and B, and two service cost centres, stores and the canteen.

The budgeted overheads for the next period are as follows:

	Total £	A £	B £	Stores £	Canteen £
Indirect wages	75,700	7,800	4,700	21,200	42,000
Rent	24,000				
Buildings insurance	2,000				
Power	6,400				
Heat and light	4,000				
Supervisor's wages – Dept A	10,000				
Machinery depreciation	3,200				
Machinery insurance	2,200				
Total					
Canteen					(49,730)
Stores					

You are also provided with the following information:

	Total	A	B	Stores	Canteen
Carrying value of machinery	£300,000	£140,000	£120,000	£15,000	£25,000
Power usage (%)	100%	45%	30%	5%	20%
Number of employees	126	70	40	10	6

	Total	A	B	Stores	Canteen
Supervisor's hours	40	25	15		
Floor area (sq m)	30,000	12,000	8,000	4,000	6,000
Materials requisitions	500	300	200		

The stores staff use the canteen but the canteen makes no use of the stores services.

You are required to:

(a) Allocate or apportion the overheads to each of the production and service cost centres on a fair basis and reapportion the service cost centre costs to the production cost centres using the step down method. (Work to the nearest whole £.) **(16 marks)**

Budgeted machine hours	17,000
Actual machine hours	21,250
Budgeted overheads	£85,000
Actual overheads	£110,500

(b) Based on the data above:

The machine hour absorption rate is £ [   ] per hour.

The overhead for the period was [▼] absorbed by £ [   ].

Picklist:

over-
under- **(3 marks)**

(c) The accounting entries at the end of a period for production overhead under-absorbed would be **(tick the correct boxes)**:

	Debit	Credit	No entry in this a/c
Overhead control account			
Production account			
Statement of profit or loss			

(2 marks)

(d) The overhead absorption rate for product M is £8 per machine hour. Each unit of M requires 1 machine hour. Inventories of product M last period were:

	Units
Opening inventory	6,000
Closing inventory	6,750

The absorption costing profit for the period for product M will be:

☐ higher

☐ lower   (1 mark)

than the marginal costing profit. The difference between the two profit figures will be

£ [   ]   (2 marks)

Task 3 (24 marks)

This task is about short-term decision making.

(a) Identify whether the following statements are true or false.

Statement	True ✓	False ✓
Contribution is associated with absorption costing.		
Contribution equals sales less variable costs.		

(2 marks)

(b) JLS Ltd operates a job costing system. The company calculates the cost of the job and then adds 20% profit onto the cost to produce a sales price.

The estimated costs for job EIL are as follows.

Direct materials   3 kg @ £5 per kg

Direct labour   4 hours @ £9 per hour

Production overheads are budgeted to be £240,000 for the period and are absorbed on the basis of a total of 30,000 labour hours.

Fill in the table below to calculate the selling price for the job.

Job EIL	£
Direct materials	
Direct labour	
Production overheads	
Total cost	
20% profit	
Selling price for the job	

(8 marks)

BPP LEARNING MEDIA

(c)   ABF Co is a company producing and selling two types of toys: the elephant and the giraffe. The expected monthly costs and sales information for each toy is as follows.

Toy	Elephant	Giraffe
Sales and production quantity	1,250	1,750
Labour hours per month	120	100
Total sales revenue	£2,500	£3,500
Total direct materials	£200	£350
Total direct labour	£750	£875
Total variable overheads	£50	£140

The total expected monthly fixed costs relating to the production of all toys is £750.

(i)   You are required to complete the table below to show the profit volume ratio for each toy.

Toy	Elephant £	Giraffe £
Selling price per toy		
Less: Unit variable costs		
Direct materials		
Direct labour		
Variable overheads		
Contribution per toy		
Profit volume ratio (%)		

(10 marks)

(ii)   ABF has decided stop making elephant toys. The expected monthly fixed costs remain at £750. Calculate the breakeven point to the nearest whole unit.

[   ] units   (2 marks)

(iii) Calculate the margin of safety.

[   ] units   (2 marks)

Task 4 (16 marks)

This task is about understanding the principles of budgeting and cash management.

(a)   (i)   Which of the following is the correct description of a flexible budget?

	✓
A budget that cannot be adjusted	
A budget that is adjusted according to actual activity	
A budget that is adjusted according to planned activity	
A budget that cannot be used to calculate variances	

(2 marks)

(ii)   The following is taken from the production cost budget of Oscarr Ltd.

Production units	2,000	3,000
Production cost	£11,100	£12,900

What is the budgeted cost for an activity level of 4,000 units?

	✓
£7,200	
£7,500	
£13,460	
£14,700	

(2 marks)

(iii)   Which of the following is a way of improving operational cash flows in a business?

	✓
Taking more credit from suppliers	
Giving more credit to customers	
Increasing inventory	
Taking advantage of early settlement discounts from suppliers	

(2 marks)

(iv)   Cash forecasts are likely to show which TWO of the following?

	✓
How much cash is required	
Profit	
When cash is required	
The sources of funding available	

(2 marks)

(b) The following information is available for Jaspie Ltd:

Year end	31 December 20X1
Revenue	3,250,600
Cost of sales	1,987,400
Trade receivables	386,500
Trade payables	328,400
Inventory	190,950

Complete the table below for Jaspie Ltd to show the working capital cycle for the year ended 31 December 20X1. Enter answers to the nearest whole day and as positive figures.

	31 December 20X1 Days
Trade receivables collection period	
Trade payables payment period	
Inventory holding period	
Working capital cycle	

(8 marks)

Task 5 (16 marks)

This task is about the preparation of budgets.

You have been given a spreadsheet **Inventory.xls** which shows inventory held at a distribution centre. It contains four worksheets: 'Inventory list', 'Location', 'Price List' and 'Order June 20X6'.

Download this spreadsheet file from www.bpp.com/aatspreadsheets and save in the appropriate location. Rename it using the following format: **'your initial-surname-AAT no –dd.mm.yy-Task5'.**

For example: J-Donnovan-123456-12.03xx-Task5

A **high degree of accuracy** is required. You **must save your work as an .XLS or .XLSX file** at regular intervals to avoid losing your work.

(a) (i) Open the inventory list worksheet and use lookup functions to complete:

   • The location code information in Column B   (2 marks)

   • The unit price information in Column C   (2 marks)

   • Insert a formula to calculate the value of each item of inventory in Column E   (1 mark)

(ii) Insert a function to determine whether or not items are due to be re-ordered in Column G.

   • If the item is above the re-order level, this should return the value 0. If the item is on or under the re-order level, this should return the value 1.

(2 marks)

(iii) Format the data contained in cells B1:H22 as a table, using Table style medium 14

- Format cells A1:A22 using the fill function to change the cell colour to blue grey, accent 6, darker 25%, and change the font colour to white to make it more visible. (2 marks)

- Hide the gridlines to improve the look of the worksheet. (1 mark)

- Sort the data by using the filter on column H to remove all items that have been discontinued. (1 mark)

- Hide Column H. (1 mark)

(iv) Use the filter function to show only those items that need to be reordered. (2 marks)

- Copy and paste the relevant items on to the Order June 20X6 worksheet to create an order list. (2 marks)

- Ensure you do not copy over the table format to the new order list.

Task 6

This task is about budgets and deviations.

Figures for the original budget and actual performance for Jumbo Ltd have been entered into the spreadsheet. The original budget now needs to be flexed.

(a) Complete the following in the 'Flexed budget' worksheet:

Direct costs are variable costs, but the overheads are fixed.

(i) In cell D1 use a formula to calculate the percentage by which to flex the original budget. (1 mark)

(ii) Format cell D1 as a percentage. (1 mark)

(iii) In cells D10:D14 create a flexed budget. Use formulas to flex the revenue, costs and operating profit. Where necessary, use absolute referencing. (4 marks)

(iv) In cells E10:E14 calculate the variances for sales, each cost, and operating profit. Show adverse variances as negative numbers with a minus sign. (4 marks)

(v) Use data validation to restrict entries in cells F10:F14, allowing only the contents of cells A1:A2 in the 'List' worksheet. (1 mark)

(vi) In cells F10:F14 indicate whether each variance is Favourable or Adverse by entering F or A. If neither F nor A enter 0. (4 marks)

Jumbo Ltd has a policy of investigating any variances that are over 20% of the flexed budget amount.

(vii) In cells E10:E13, highlight in yellow any variances which need to be investigated. (1 mark)

BPP Practice Assessment 2 Management Accounting Techniques

Answers

BPP
LEARNING
MEDIA

Management Accounting Techniques (MATS)
BPP Practice Assessment 2

Task 1

(a) (i)

	✓
The action of monitoring something to keep it on course.	✓
The choice between alternatives.	
The development of strategies to achieve objectives.	
The establishment of a plan for a future period.	

The choice between alternatives is decision making. The development of strategies and establishment of a plan are planning.

(ii)

	✓
Batch costing	
Job costing	✓
Unit costing	
Service costing	

Job costing is most appropriate when production is carried out in accordance with the special requirements of each customer.

(iii)

Account	DR ✓	CR ✓
Finished goods	✓	
Production		✓

(b) (i)   £ 5,200

(ii)   £ 7,300

(iii) £ 8,150

(iv)   £ 0.09

(v)   £ 0.10

(vi)

	✓
Marginal costs	✓
Period costs	
Prime costs	
Product costs	

(c) (i)

	✓
(i) and (iv) only	
(ii) and (iv) only	
(ii), (iii) and (iv) only	✓
All of them	

Statement (i) is not correct. A debit to materials with a corresponding credit to production indicates that direct materials returned from production were £45,000.

Statement (ii) is correct. Direct costs of production are 'collected' in the production account.

Statement (iii) is correct. Indirect costs of production or overhead are 'collected' in the overhead control account.

Statement (iv) is correct. The purchases of materials on credit are credited to the payables account and debited to the inventory account.

(ii) $EOQ = \sqrt{\dfrac{2cd}{h}}$

(iii)

	✓
Stores credit note	
Stores debit note	
Materials returned note	✓
Materials transfer note	

BPP LEARNING MEDIA

Task 2

(a)

	Total £	A £	B £	Stores £	Canteen £
Indirect wages	75,700	7,800	4,700	21,200	42,000
Rent	24,000	9,600	6,400	3,200	4,800
Buildings insurance	2,000	800	533	267	400
Power	6,400	2,880	1,920	320	1,280
Heat and light	4,000	1,600	1,067	533	800
Supervisor's wages	10,000	10,000	–	–	–
Machinery depreciation	3,200	1,493	1,280	160	267
Machinery insurance	2,200	1,027	880	110	183
Total	127,500	35,200	16,780	25,790	49,730
Canteen		29,009	16,577	4,144	(49,730)
				29,934	
Stores		17,960	11,974	(29,934)	
		82,169	45,331	–	–

Workings:

Rent, buildings insurance and heat and light are apportioned on the basis of floor area – 12:8:4:6.

Power is apportioned using the percentages given.

Supervisor's wages are allocated directly to department A.

Machinery depreciation and insurance are apportioned on the basis of the net book value of the machinery – 140:120:15:25.

Canteen costs are apportioned according to the number of staff that use it – 70:40:10.

The stores costs are apportioned on the basis of the number of materials requisitions.

(b) The machine hour absorption rate is £ [5] per hour.

$$\text{Overhead absorption rate} = \frac{\text{Budgeted overheads}}{\text{Budgeted machine hours}}$$

$$= \frac{£85,000}{17,000}$$

$$= £5$$

The overhead for the period was [under] absorbed by £ [4,250].

Overhead over-/(under)-absorbed = Overhead absorbed – Overhead incurred

$$= (21,250 \times £5) - £110,500$$

$$= £(4,250)$$

(c)

	Debit £	Credit £	No entry in this a/c £
Overhead control account		✓	
Production account			✓
Statement of profit or loss	✓		

Under-absorbed overhead means that the overhead charged to production was too low and so there must be a debit to the statement of profit or loss.

(d)   The absorption costing profit for the period for product M will be:

✓   higher

than the marginal costing profit. The difference between the two profit figures will be

£ | 6,000

Difference in profit = change in inventory level × fixed overhead per unit

$$= (6,000 - 6,750) \times (£8 \times 1)$$

$$= £6,000$$

The absorption costing profit will be higher because inventories have increased, and fixed overheads have been carried forward in inventory.

Task 3

(a)

Statement	True ✓	False ✓
Contribution is associated with absorption costing.		✓
Contribution equals sales less variable costs.	✓	

(b)

Job EIL	£
Direct materials (3 kg × £5)	15.00
Direct labour (4 hours × £9)	36.00
Production overheads (4 hours × £8)*	32.00
Total production cost	83.00
20% profit (£83.00 × 0.2)	16.60
Selling price for the job	99.60

$$* \text{ OAR} = \frac{£240,000}{30,000} = £8 \text{ per labour hour}$$

(c) (i)

Toy	Elephant £	Giraffe £
Selling price per toy (W1)	2.00	2.00
Less: Unit variable costs		
Direct materials (W2)	0.16	0.20
Direct labour (W3)	0.60	0.50
Variable overheads (W4)	0.04	0.08
Contribution per toy*	1.20	1.22
Profit volume ratio (%)**	60%	61%

* Contribution = Selling price – Variable costs

** Profit volume ratio = Contribution ÷ selling price × 100%

Workings:

1   Selling price per bottle

$$\text{Selling price per toy} = \frac{\text{Total sales revenue}}{\text{Sales (toys)}}$$

$$\text{Elephant} = \frac{£2,500}{1,250} = £2 \text{ per toy}$$

$$\text{Giraffe} = \frac{£3,500}{1,750} = £2 \text{ per toy}$$

2   Direct materials per toy

$$\text{Direct materials per toy} = \frac{\text{Total direct material costs}}{\text{Production volume}}$$

$$\text{Elephant} = \frac{£200}{1,250} = £0.16 \text{ per toy}$$

$$\text{Giraffe} = \frac{£350}{1,750} = £0.20 \text{ per toy}$$

3   Direct labour cost per toy

$$\text{Direct labour cost per toy} = \frac{\text{Total direct labour costs}}{\text{Production volume}}$$

$$\text{Elephant} = \frac{£750}{1,250} = £0.60 \text{ per toy}$$

$$\text{Giraffe} = \frac{£875}{1,750} = £0.50 \text{ per toy}$$

4   Variable overheads per toy

$$\text{Variable overheads per toy} = \frac{\text{Total variable overhead costs}}{\text{Production volume}}$$

$$\text{Elephant} = \frac{£50}{1,250} = £0.04 \text{ per toy}$$

BPP LEARNING MEDIA

$$\text{Giraffe} = \frac{£140}{1,750} = £0.08 \text{ per toy}$$

(ii) Breakeven point = Fixed costs/Contribution per unit

= £750/1.22

= 615 units (to the nearest unit)

(iii) Margin of safety = Budgeted sales units – breakeven sales units

= 1,750 – 615

= 1,135

Task 4

(a) (i) Which of the following is the correct description of a flexible budget?

	✓
A budget that cannot be adjusted	
A budget that is adjusted according to actual activity	✓
A budget that is adjusted according to planned activity	
A budget that cannot be used to calculate variances	

(ii)

	✓
£7,200	
£7,500	
£13,460	
£14,700	✓

Using the high low method, the variable cost per unit = (£12,900 – £11,100)/(3,000 – 2,000) = £1.80 per unit

Therefore fixed cost = £12,900 – (3,000 × £1.80) = £7,500

The budgeted cost for 4,000 units = £7,500 + (£1.80 × 4,000) = £14,700

(iii)

	✓
Taking more credit from suppliers	✓
Giving more credit to customers	
Increasing inventory	
Taking advantage of early settlement discounts from suppliers	

(iv)

	✓
How much cash is required	✓
Profit	
When cash is required	✓
The sources of funding available	

(b)

	31 December 20X1 Days
Trade receivables collection period	43
Trade payables payment period	60
Inventory holding period	35
Working capital cycle	18

Trade receivables collection period = trade receivables / revenue × 365 days = 386,500 / 3,250,600 × 365 days = 43 days

Trade payables payment period = trade payables / cost of sales × 365 days = 328,400 / 1,987,400 × 365 days = 60 days

Inventory holding period = Inventory / cost of sales × 365 days = 190,950 / 1,987,400 × 365 days = 35 days

Working capital cycle = 43 − 60 + 35 = 18

Task 5

- Open the inventory list worksheet and use lookup functions to complete.

    - The location code information in Column B.

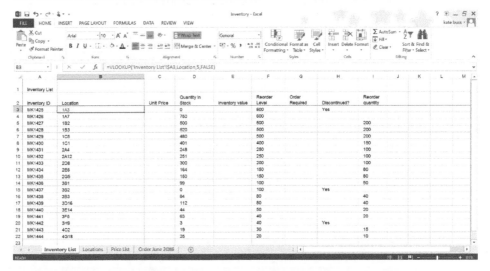

- The unit price information in Column C.

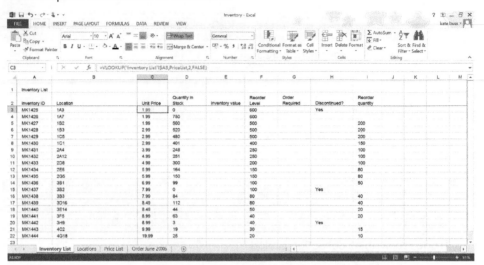

- Insert a formula to calculate the value of each item of inventory in Column E.

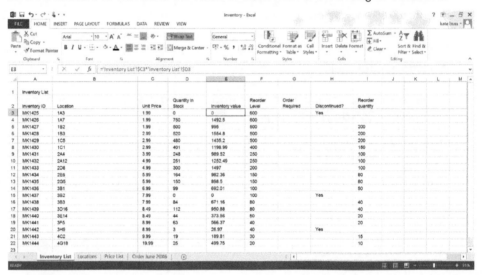

- Insert an IF function to determine whether or not items are due to be re-ordered in Column G.

  - If the item is above the re-order level, this should return the value 0. If the item is on or under the re-order level, this should return the value 1.

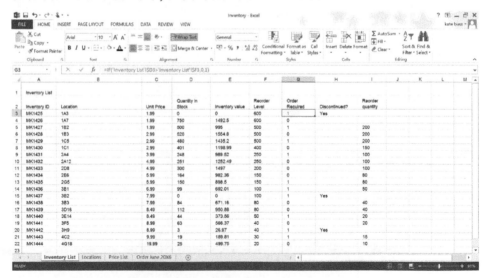

- Format the data contained in cells B1:H22 as a table, using Table style medium 14.
  - Format cells A1:A22 using the fill function to change the cell colour to blue grey, accent 6, darker 25% and change the font colour to white to make it more visible.
  - Hide the gridlines to improve the look of the worksheet.

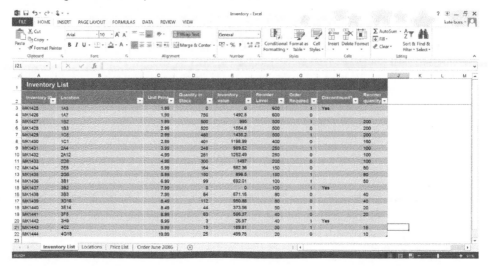

- Sort the data by using the filter on Column H to remove all items that have been discontinued.

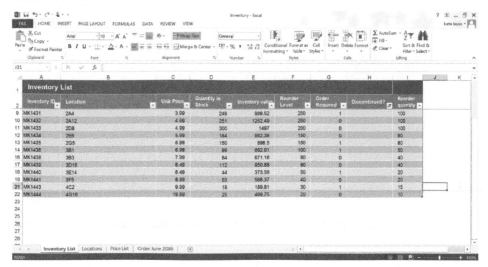

- Hide Column H.

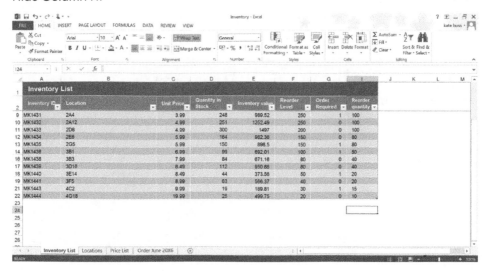

- Use the filter function to show only those items that need to be reordered.

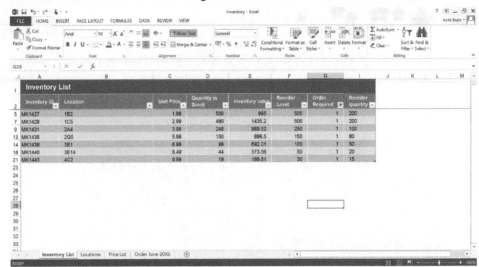

Step 1. Copy and paste the relevant items on to the Order June 20X6 worksheet to create an order list.

Step 2. Ensure you do not copy over the table format to the new order list.

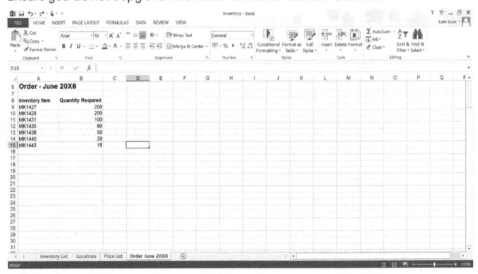

Task 6

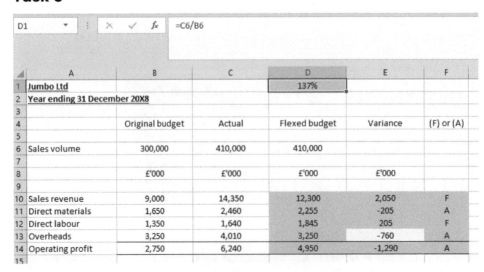

D1 | fx | =C6/B6

Jumbo Ltd
Year ending 31 December 20X8

	A	B	C	D	E	F
1	Jumbo Ltd			137%		
2	Year ending 31 December 20X8					
3						
4		Original budget	Actual	Flexed budget	Variance	(F) or (A)
5						
6	Sales volume	300,000	410,000	410,000		
7						
8		£'000	£'000	£'000	£'000	
9						
10	Sales revenue	9,000	14,350	12,300	2,050	F
11	Direct materials	1,650	2,460	2,255	-205	A
12	Direct labour	1,350	1,640	1,845	205	F
13	Overheads	3,250	4,010	3,250	-760	A
14	Operating profit	2,750	6,240	4,950	-1,290	A
15						

BPP LEARNING MEDIA

BPP Practice Assessment 3

Management Accounting Techniques

Time allowed: 2 hours 30 minutes

Management Accounting Techniques (MATS)
BPP Practice Assessment 3

Task 1 (24 marks)

This task is about costing techniques.

(a) Drag and drop the correct entries into the journal below to record the following FOUR accounting transactions:

Receipt of metal widgets into inventory paying by BACS
Issue of metal widgets from inventory to production
Receipt of metal widgets into inventory paying on credit
Return of metal widgets from production to inventory

The drag and drop choices are:

Debit Inventory, Credit Trade payables control
Debit Inventory, Credit Production
Debit Inventory, Credit Bank
Debit Bank, Credit Goods inward
Debit Trade payables control, Credit Goods inward
Debit Production, Credit Inventory

	Drag and drop choice
Transaction 1	
Transaction 2	
Transaction 3	
Transaction 4	

(4 marks)

Tagus Ltd had the following receipts of inventory in June.

Date purchased	Quantity	Cost per kg	Total cost £
22 June	500	1.250	625
24 June	392	1.305	511.56

400 kg were issued to production on 26 June.

(b) Drag and drop the correct cost into the cost column of the table below to record the issue on 26 June and to record the inventory balance after the issue using FIFO (first in, first out).

	Cost
FIFO issue	
FIFO balance	

£1,136.56	£636.56
£625	£500

(2 marks)

Bynlu Ltd has started working on a new type of pencil. At the start of June, the work in progress was valued at £30,000 and the other costs during the month were:

	£
Materials	13,500
Labour	78,000
Production overhead	60,500

(c) (i) What is the total cost of production to date for the pencils?

£ [   ]

(1 mark)

At the end of the month, 6,080 units were fully complete and there was a total closing work in progress of 1,200 units which were 85% complete.

(ii) What are the equivalent units of production of the closing work in progress?

[   ] units

(1 mark)

(iii) Calculate the closing value of work in progress of the pencils.

£ [   ]

(2 marks)

(d) Drag and drop the correct answers into the table below:

1. Prime cost
2. Materials
3. Production overheads
4. Production costs
5. Non-production overheads
6. Total cost

(6 marks)

BPP
LEARNING
MEDIA

(e) There are three main methods of costing – absorption costing, marginal costing and activity based costing (ABC).

Drag and drop the correct answers into the boxes below:

1. Absorption costing
2. Marginal costing
3. Activity based costing

[dropdown ▼] is where the production overheads are included in full in the cost of each unit.

[dropdown ▼] is where only variable overheads are included in the cost of each unit with the fixed overheads being charged to the income statement as a period cost.

(2 marks)

(f) You have been presented with the following figures relating to the accounts of Zenco Ltd which manufactures pharmaceuticals.

Figures for year ended 31 Dec 20X1

	£
Revenue from sales	350,000
Raw materials	62,300
Production: site rent and rates	9,400
Production: staff wages	72,780
Production: supervisors' wages	32,560
Licence payments to produce goods	5,100
Administration offices rent and rates	3,750
Administration staff salaries	37,600
Depreciation: production machinery	6,860
Depreciation: general office equipment	2,700
Other expenses: production	3,450
Other expenses: administration	1,230

Calculate the following and insert your answer in the box provided:

1. Prime cost   £ [   ]

2. Production cost   £ [   ]

3. Total cost   £ [   ]

(6 marks)

Task 2 (24 marks)

This task is about attributing costs.

Emsam Ltd's budgeted overheads for the next financial year are:

	£	£
Machinery leasing costs		1,020,000
Rent and rates		1,058,400
Light and heat		231,840
Indirect labour costs:		
Canteen	45,400	
Maintenance	30,455	
Total indirect labour		75,855

The following information is also available:

Department	Carrying value of machinery	Floor space (square metres)	Number of employees
Production cost centres:			
Component manufacturing	5,600,000	48,000	17
Assembly	2,400,000	30,000	12
Support cost centres:			
Canteen		5,000	3
Maintenance			1
Total	8,000,000	83,000	33

- Overheads are allocated or apportioned on the most appropriate basis. The total overheads of the support cost centres are then reapportioned to the two production centres.

- The canteen costs are reapportioned on the basis of number of employees (17, 12 and 1).

- The Maintenance department's time is split between the Component manufacturing and Assembly departments in proportion to the carrying value of the department's machinery.

- All employees use the canteen.

(a) Complete the table showing the apportionment and reapportionment of overheads to the two production centres:

	Basis of apportionment	Component manufacturing £	Assembly £	Canteen £	Maintenance £	Totals £
Machinery leasing costs	Carrying value of machinery					
Rent and rates	Floor space					
Light and heat	Floor space					
Indirect labour	Allocated					
Totals						

	Basis of apportionment	Component manufacturing £	Assembly £	Canteen £	Maintenance £	Totals £
Reapportion Canteen						
Subtotal						
Reapportion Maintenance						
Total overheads to production centres						

(15 marks)

In the following year, Emsam Ltd's canteen equipment is likely to need regular maintenance which means there will be reciprocal work between the service departments.

(b) **What impact will this have on the method used to apportion overheads to production cost centres?**

	✓
The Maintenance department will need an additional employee whose salary can be allocated to the Canteen cost centre.	
Some of the Maintenance overheads will be apportioned to the Canteen so the step-down method of reapportionment will be more appropriate.	
Both service departments will be working for all other departments so their overheads can be split evenly between them.	
No impact.	

(2 marks)

Emsam Ltd are considering introducing activity based costing (ABC) and have analysed their production overheads for the next quarter into cost pools.

(c) Which cost driver would be most appropriate to use in the calculation of overhead recovery rates for each of these cost pools?

	Cost driver
Raw material handing	▼
Set-up costs	▼
Machine maintenance	▼

Picklist:

Labour hours
Machine hours
Production runs
Supplier deliveries
Units of production

(3 marks)

(d) Which of the following would be the most appropriate basis for apportionment of motor vehicle overheads for a courier company?

	✓
Labour hours	
Parcels delivered	
Miles driven	
Customer orders	

(2 marks)

(e) Select the correct statement:

☐ Under-absorbed overheads will be debited to the statement of profit or loss

☐ Under-absorbed overheads will be credited to the statement of profit or loss

(2 marks)

Task 3 (24 marks)

This task is about short-term decision making.

Lisboa Ltd has prepared a forecast for the next quarter for one of its small plastic components, ZEST. This component is produced in batches and the forecast is based on selling and producing 2,400 batches.

One of the customers of Lisboa Ltd has indicated that it may be significantly increasing its order level for component ZEST for the next quarter and it appears that activity levels of 3,500 batches and 4,000 batches are feasible.

The semi-variable costs should be calculated using the high-low method. If 6,000 batches are sold the total semi-variable cost will be £14,754, and there is a constant unit variable cost up to this volume.

BPP LEARNING MEDIA

(a) Complete the table below and calculate the estimated profit per batch of ZEST at the different activity levels: (Work to the nearest whole number until the profit per batch.)

| Batches produced and sold | 2,400 | 3,500 | 4,000 |
	£	£	£
Sales revenue	45,500	66,354	
Variable costs:			
Direct materials	11,250		18,750
Direct labour	10,850		
Overheads	6,825	9,953	
Semi-variable costs:	8,400		
Variable element			
Fixed element			
Total cost	37,325	52,524	
Total profit	8,175		16,401
Profit per batch (to 2 decimal places)	3.41		

(12 marks)

Product TEST has a selling price of £32 per unit with a total variable cost of £24 per unit. Avignon Ltd estimates that the fixed costs per quarter associated with this product are £43,000.

(b) (i) Calculate the budgeted breakeven, in units, for product TEST.

[　　　　　　　] units (2 marks)

(ii) Calculate the budgeted breakeven, in £s, for product TEST.

£ [　　　　　　　]

(2 marks)

(iii) Complete the table below to show the budgeted margin of safety in units and the margin of safety percentage if Avignon Ltd sells 5,500 units or 7,000 units of product TEST:

| Units of TEST sold | 5,500 | 7,000 |
	£	£
Margin of safety (units)		
Margin of safety percentage (nearest whole percentage)		

(4 marks)

(iv) If Avignon Ltd wishes to make a profit of £35,000, how many units of TEST must it sell?

[　　　　　　　] units (2 marks)

(v) If Avignon Ltd decreases the selling price of TEST by 10p what will be the impact on the breakeven point and the margin of safety, assuming no change in the number of units sold?

	✓
The breakeven point will decrease and the margin of safety will increase.	
The breakeven point will stay the same but the margin of safety will decrease.	
The breakeven point will increase and the margin of safety will decrease.	
The breakeven point will increase and the margin of safety stay the same.	

(2 marks)

Task 4 (16 marks)

This task is about understanding the principles of budgeting and of cash management.

(a) Which one of the following equations best describes the working capital cycle?

☐ Average inventory holding period + average trade payables payment period – average trade receivables collection period

☐ Average inventory holding period + average trade receivables collection period – average trade payables payment period

☐ Average cash balance + average trade receivables collection period – average trade payables payment period

☐ Average cash balance – average trade receivables collection period + average trade payables payment period

(1 mark)

(b) Which of the following should a business do in order to improve its cash operating cycle?

☐ Increase inventories of raw material

☐ Decrease the credit period taken from trade suppliers

☐ Extend the credit period for customers

☐ Reduce the time taken to produce its product

(1 mark)

(c) A company's current cash operating cycle is 34 days.

Which of the following will have the effect of reducing the cash operating cycle?

☐ Increasing the inventory holding period by 3 days

☐ Decreasing the trade payables' payment period by 5 days

☐ Decreasing the trade receivables' collection period by 2 days

☐ Increasing the average cash balance by 10%

(1 mark)

(d)   Identify, by selecting Add or Deduct, how a business reconciles profit with cash.

Add ✓	Deduct ✓	Profit
		Depreciation
		Sale of non-current assets
		Injection of funds from new loan
		Drawings
		= Cash

(4 marks)

(e)   A car manufacturer is considering purchasing a new paint-spraying machine which would replace the paint-spraying workforce. Which of the following options would NOT be a suitable funding method for the acquisition of this non-current asset?

	✓
Cash	
Hire purchase	
Loan	
Part exchange	

(1 mark)

(f)   You have been asked to calculate the working capital cycle of a business.

Extracts from the financial statements are shown below.

Statement of profit or loss	£
Revenue	1,652,877
Cost of sales	512,011

Statement of financial position	£
Trade receivables	197,760
Trade payables	81,979
Inventory	175,208

Complete the table below to show the working capital cycle. Enter answers to the nearest whole day and as positive figures.

	Days
Inventory holding period	
Receivables collection period	
Payables payment period	
Working capital cycle	

(8 marks)

Task 5 (16 marks)

This task is about the preparation of budgets.

You have been given a spreadsheet **PA3 Task 5 Damat.xls** which contains two worksheets: 'Original budget' and 'Actual results'.

Download this spreadsheet file from www.bpp.com/aatspreadsheets and save in the appropriate location. Rename it using the following format: **'your initial-surname-AAT no –dd.mm.yy-Damat'**.

For example: J-Donnovan-123456-12.03xx-Damat

A **high degree of accuracy** is required. You **must save your work as an .XLS or .XLSX file** at regular intervals to avoid losing your work.

Damat Ltd are a garden landscaping company who have several large contracts with local housing associations as well as smaller regular customers.

The owners of the business are concerned that the results for the first month of the year are worse than expected and would like you to help prepare a rolling budget.

It is now 31 January 20X1.

(a) Open the renamed spreadsheet and complete the following in the 'Original budget' worksheet.

(i) Format cells A1 to A3 bold and underlined. (1 mark)

(ii) In row 11 (from cell B11 to cell M11) calculate the monthly profit using an appropriate formula and the total in cell N11. (1 mark)

(iii) Format cells B11 to N11 with a top and bottom border. (1 mark)

(iv) Format row 11 to be bold. (1 mark)

(b) Create a copy of the 'Original budget' worksheet and name the new worksheet 'Rolling budget'. The new worksheet should be located to the right of the 'Actual results'. (1 mark)

(c) Investigations into the actual results for January have revealed the following information:

- Damat lost one of their large contracts at the end of December 20X0 and this has not been reflected in the original budget for 20X1. This contract was for £2,500 per month.

- Variable materials are 9% of revenue and labour is 45% of revenue.

- From July 20X1, fixed overheads are due to increase by 2%. This has not been reflected in the original budget for 20X1.

Complete the following in the new 'Rolling budget' worksheet.

(i)   Change the heading in cell A3 to 'Rolling budget' and change the heading in cell B5 to 'Jan actual'.   (1 mark)

(ii)   Link the cells in column B (from cell B7 to cell B10) to the appropriate cells in the 'Actual results' worksheet to enter the actual results for January into the rolling budget.   (2 marks)

(iii)   In row 7 (from cell C7 to cell M7), delete the current figures and use an appropriate formula to link the revenue figures for February to December to the 'Original budget' worksheet and adjust the formula to deduct the lost contract.   (2 marks)

(iv)   In rows 8 and 9 (from cell C8 to cell M9) calculate the variable materials and variable labour costs, using appropriate formulas.   (2 marks)

(v)   In row 10 (from cell C10 to cell M10) use an appropriate formula to link the fixed overheads figures to the 'Original budget' worksheet and adjust the formula to calculate the inflated cost in the appropriate months.   (2 marks)

(vi)   Change the orientation of the page to landscape and set the print area to cell A1 to cell N11.   (2 marks)

Task 6 (16 marks)

This task is about budgets and deviations.

You have been given a spreadsheet **PA3 Task 6 Clarkson.xls**.

Download this spreadsheet file from www.bpp.com/aatspreadsheets and save in the appropriate location. Rename it using the following format: **'your initial-surname-AAT no –dd.mm.yy-Clarkson'**.

For example: J-Donnovan-123456-12.03xx-Clarkson

A **high degree of accuracy** is required. You **must save your work as an .XLS or .XLSX file** at regular intervals to avoid losing your work.

Clarkson Ltd manufacture and sell pet accessories.

The budgeted and actual results for the past year have been entered into the spreadsheet.

(a)   Complete the following in the renamed spreadsheet.

(i)   In cell C4, use an appropriate formula to calculate the percentage by which the budget should be flexed to reflect the actual sales volume.   (1 mark)

(ii)   Format cell C4 to show a percentage to one decimal place.   (1 mark)

(iii)   In column C (from cell C8 to cell C11) calculate the flexed budget. Use formulas to flex the revenue and costs, using absolute referencing where necessary.
                                                                              (5 marks)

(iv)   In column E (from cell E8 to cell E12) calculate the variances for revenue, each cost and profit, using appropriate formulas. Enter all figures as positive numbers.   (2 marks)

(v)   In column F (from cell F8 to cell F12) calculate the variances as a percentage of the flexed budget.   (2 marks)

(vi)   Identify which variances are adverse by formatting the relevant cells in column F as red font.   (2 marks)

(vii)   Format cells B12 to F12 as bold with a top and double bottom border.   (1 mark)

(viii)   Insert a 2D column chart underneath the data using the data range
         A8:A11,E8:E11   (1 mark)

(ix)   Add a chart title 'Variances' at the top of the chart.   (1 mark)

BPP Practice Assessment 3

Management Accounting Techniques

Answers

Management Accounting Techniques (MATS)
BPP Practice Assessment 3

Task 1

(a)

	Drag and drop choice
Transaction 1	Debit Inventory, Credit Bank
Transaction 2	Debit Production, Credit Inventory
Transaction 3	Debit Inventory, Credit Trade payables' control
Transaction 4	Debit Inventory, Credit Production

(b)

	Cost
FIFO issue	£500.00
FIFO balance	£636.56

Workings:

FIFO issue = 400 kg × £1.250 = £500

FIFO balance = (100 kg × £1.250) + (392 kg × £1.305) = £636.56

(c) (i)

£ 182,000

£30,000 + £13,500 + £78,000 + £60,500 = £182,000

(ii)

1,020 units

1,200 units × 85% = 1,020 units

(iii)

£ 25,500

Cost per equivalent unit = £182,000 / (6,080 + 1,200) = £25

Value of closing WIP = £25 × 1,020 = £25,500

(d)

```
┌─────────────────────────────────────────────────────────┐
│ COST CARD                                                 │
│                                                      £    │
│          ┌──────────────────┐                            │
│ Direct   │    Materials     │                       X    │
│          └──────────────────┘                            │
│ Direct labour                                        X    │
│ Direct expenses                                      X    │
│                                                     ───   │
│          ┌──────────────────┐                       X    │
│          │    Prime cost    │                            │
│          └──────────────────┘                            │
│        ┌───────────────────────┐                         │
│        │ Production overheads  │                    X    │
│        └───────────────────────┘                   ───   │
│        ┌──────────────────┐                         X    │
│        │ Production cost  │                              │
│        └──────────────────┘                              │
│      ┌──────────────────────────┐                        │
│      │ Non-production overheads │                        │
│      └──────────────────────────┘                        │
│        –    selling and distribution                X    │
│        –    administration                          X    │
│        –    finance                                 X    │
│                                                     ───   │
│          ┌──────────────────┐                       X    │
│          │    Total cost    │                      ═══   │
│          └──────────────────┘                            │
└─────────────────────────────────────────────────────────┘
```

(e)   **Absorption costing** is where the production overheads are included in full in the cost of each unit.

Marginal costing is where only variable overheads are included in the cost of each unit with the fixed overheads being charged to the income statement as a period cost.

(f)   **Total cost statement for Zenco for the year ended 31ˢᵗ Dec 20X1**

	£	£
Direct materials		62,300
Direct labour		72,780
Direct expenses		5,100
PRIME COST		140,180
Production overheads		
Production site rent and rates	9,400	
Production: supervisors' wages	32,560	
Depreciation: production machinery	6,860	
Other expenses: Production	3,450	52,270
PRODUCTION COST		192,450

BPP
LEARNING
MEDIA

	£	£
Non-production overheads		
Depreciation: general office equipment	2,700	
Administration staff salaries	37,600	
Administration offices rent and rates	3,750	
Other expenses: Administration	1,230	45,280
TOTAL COST		237,730

Task 2

(a)

	Basis of apportionment	Component manufacturing £	Assembly £	Canteen £	Maintenance £	Totals £
Machinery leasing costs	Carrying value of machinery	714,000	306,000			1,020,000
Rent and rates	Floor space	612,087	382,554	63,759		1,058,400
Light and heat	Floor space	134,076	83,798	13,966		231,840
Indirect labour	Allocated			45,400	30,455	75,855
Totals		1,460,163	772,352	123,125	30,455	2,386,095

	Basis of apportionment	Component manufacturing £	Assembly £	Canteen £	Maintenance £	Totals £
Reapportion Canteen*		69,771	49,250	(123,125)	4,104	
Subtotal		1,529,934	821,602	0	34,559	2,386,095
Reapportion Maintenance		24,191	10,368		(34,559)	
Total overheads to production centres		1,554,125	831,970			2,386,095

* 17 + 12 + 1 = 30 employees.

Component manufacturing: [(17/30) × £123,125] = £69,771

Assembly: [(12/30) × £123,125] = £49,250

Maintenance: [(1/30) × £123,125] = £4,104

(b) The correct answer is: Some of the Maintenance overheads will be apportioned to the Canteen so the step-down method of reapportionment will be more appropriate.

(c)

	Cost driver
Raw material handing	Supplier deliveries
Set-up costs	Production runs
Machine maintenance	Machine hours

(d) The correct answer is: Miles driven

(e) The correct statement is **under-absorbed overheads will be debited to the statement of profit or loss** as not enough overheads have been charged to the statement of profit or loss.

Task 3

(a)

Batches produced and sold	2,400	3,500	4,000
	£	£	£
Sales revenue	45,500	66,354	75,833
Variable costs:			
Direct materials	11,250	16,406	18,750
Direct labour	10,850	15,823	18,083
Overheads	6,825	9,953	11,375
Semi-variable costs:	8,400		
Variable element		6,178	7,060
Fixed element		4,164	4,164
Total cost	37,325	52,524	59,432
Total profit	8,175	13,830	16,401
Profit per batch (to 2 decimal places)	3.41	3.95	4.10

(b) (i) 5,375 units

(ii) £ 172,000

(iii)

Units of TEST sold	5,500	7,000
	£	£
Margin of safety (units)	125	1,625
Margin of safety percentage	2%	23%

BPP LEARNING MEDIA

(iv)

| 9,750 | units |

(v) The correct answer is: The breakeven point will increase and the margin of safety will decrease.

Task 4

(a) The correct answer is: Average inventory holding period + average trade receivables collection period − average trade payables payment period

(b) The correct answer is: Reduce the time taken to produce its product (as this will reduce the inventory holding period)

(c) The correct answer is: Decreasing the trade receivables' collection period by 2 days

(d)

Add ✓	Deduct ✓	Profit
✓		Depreciation
✓		Sale of non-current assets
✓		Injection of funds from new loan
	✓	Drawings
		= Cash

(e) The correct answer is: Part exchange (there is no existing machine to trade in).

(f)

	Days
Inventory holding period	175,208 / 512,011 × 365 = 125 days
Receivables collection period	197,760 / 1,652,877 × 365 = 44 days
Payables payment period	81,979 / 512,011 × 365 = 58 days
Working capital cycle	125 + 44 − 58 = 111 days

Task 5

(a)

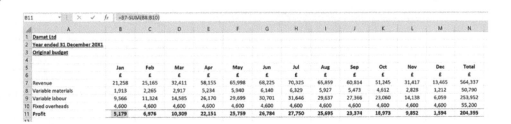

(b)

	Jan	Feb	Mar	Apr	May	Jun	Jul	Aug	Sep	Oct	Nov	Dec	Total
Damat Ltd													
Year ended 31 December 20X1													
Original budget													
	£	£	£	£	£	£	£	£	£	£	£	£	£
Revenue	21,258	25,165	32,411	58,155	65,998	68,225	70,325	65,859	60,814	51,245	31,417	13,465	564,337
Variable materials	1,913	2,265	2,917	5,234	5,940	6,140	6,329	5,927	5,473	4,612	2,828	1,212	50,790
Variable labour	9,566	11,324	14,585	26,170	29,699	30,701	31,646	29,637	27,366	23,060	14,138	6,059	253,952
Fixed overheads	4,600	4,600	4,600	4,600	4,600	4,600	4,600	4,600	4,600	4,600	4,600	4,600	55,200
Profit	5,179	6,976	10,309	22,151	25,759	26,784	27,750	25,695	23,374	18,973	9,852	1,594	204,395

Tabs: Original budget | Actual results | Rolling budget

(c)   (i) (ii)

B7   fx ='Actual results'!B7

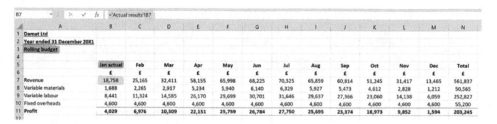

Damat Ltd
Year ended 31 December 20X1
Rolling budget

	Jan actual	Feb	Mar	Apr	May	Jun	Jul	Aug	Sep	Oct	Nov	Dec	Total
	£	£	£	£	£	£	£	£	£	£	£	£	£
Revenue	18,758	25,165	32,411	58,155	65,998	68,225	70,325	65,859	60,814	51,245	31,417	13,465	561,837
Variable materials	1,688	2,265	2,917	5,234	5,940	6,140	6,329	5,927	5,473	4,612	2,828	1,212	50,565
Variable labour	8,441	11,324	14,585	26,170	29,699	30,701	31,646	29,637	27,366	23,060	14,138	6,059	252,827
Fixed overheads	4,600	4,600	4,600	4,600	4,600	4,600	4,600	4,600	4,600	4,600	4,600	4,600	55,200
Profit	4,029	6,976	10,309	22,151	25,759	26,784	27,750	25,695	23,374	18,973	9,852	1,594	203,245

(iii)

C7   fx ='Original budget'!C7-2500

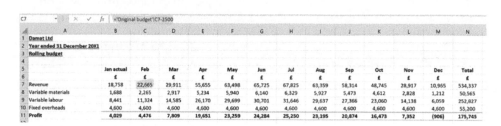

Damat Ltd
Year ended 31 December 20X1
Rolling budget

	Jan actual	Feb	Mar	Apr	May	Jun	Jul	Aug	Sep	Oct	Nov	Dec	Total
	£	£	£	£	£	£	£	£	£	£	£	£	£
Revenue	18,758	22,665	29,911	55,655	63,498	65,725	67,825	63,359	58,314	48,745	28,917	10,965	534,337
Variable materials	1,688	2,265	2,917	5,234	5,940	6,140	6,329	5,927	5,473	4,612	2,828	1,212	50,565
Variable labour	8,441	11,324	14,585	26,170	29,699	30,701	31,646	29,637	27,366	23,060	14,138	6,059	252,827
Fixed overheads	4,600	4,600	4,600	4,600	4,600	4,600	4,600	4,600	4,600	4,600	4,600	4,600	55,200
Profit	4,029	4,476	7,809	19,651	23,259	24,284	25,250	23,195	20,874	16,473	7,352	(906)	175,745

(iv)

C8   fx =C7*9%

Damat Ltd
Year ended 31 December 20X1
Rolling budget

	Jan Actual	Feb	Mar	Apr	May	Jun	Jul	Aug	Sep	Oct	Nov	Dec	Total
	£	£	£	£	£	£	£	£	£	£	£	£	£
Revenue	18,758	22,665	29,911	55,655	63,498	65,725	67,825	63,359	58,314	48,745	28,917	10,965	534,337
Variable materials	1,688	2,040	2,692	5,009	5,715	5,915	6,104	5,702	5,248	4,387	2,603	987	48,090
Variable labour	8,441	10,199	13,460	25,045	28,574	29,576	30,521	28,512	26,241	21,935	13,013	4,934	240,452
Fixed overheads	4,600	4,600	4,600	4,600	4,600	4,600	4,600	4,600	4,600	4,600	4,600	4,600	55,200
Profit	4,029	5,826	9,159	21,001	24,609	25,634	26,600	24,545	22,224	17,823	8,702	444	190,595

Note: Variable materials can also be calculated using =C7*0.09

Variable labour can be calculated using =C7*45% or =C7*0.45

(v)

H10   fx ='Original budget'!H10*1.02

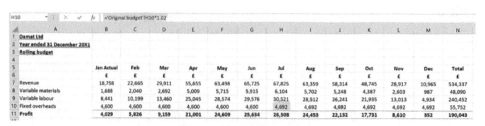

Damat Ltd
Year ended 31 December 20X1
Rolling budget

	Jan Actual	Feb	Mar	Apr	May	Jun	Jul	Aug	Sep	Oct	Nov	Dec	Total
	£	£	£	£	£	£	£	£	£	£	£	£	£
Revenue	18,758	22,665	29,911	55,655	63,498	65,725	67,825	63,359	58,314	48,745	28,917	10,965	534,337
Variable materials	1,688	2,040	2,692	5,009	5,715	5,915	6,104	5,702	5,248	4,387	2,603	987	48,090
Variable labour	8,441	10,199	13,460	25,045	28,574	29,576	30,521	28,512	26,241	21,935	13,013	4,934	240,452
Fixed overheads	4,600	4,600	4,600	4,600	4,600	4,600	4,692	4,692	4,692	4,692	4,692	4,692	55,752
Profit	4,029	5,826	9,159	21,001	24,609	25,634	26,508	24,453	22,132	17,731	8,610	352	190,043

Note: Fixed overheads for Feb-Jun should be linked to 'Original budget' without the 2% inflation.

BPP LEARNING MEDIA

(vi)

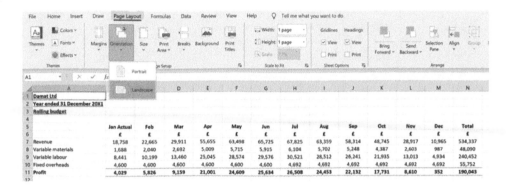

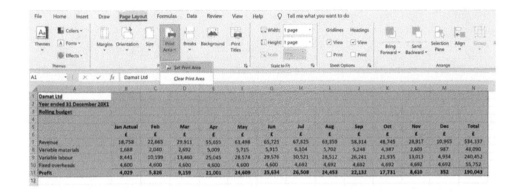

Task 6

	A	B	C	D	E	F
1	**Clarkson Ltd**					
2	**Year ended 31 March 20X4**					
3						
4			105.0%			
5		Original budget	Flexed budget	Actual results	Variance	Variance
6	Sales volume	120,000		126,000		
7		£	£	£	£	%
8	Revenue	600,000	630,000	642,600	12,600	2.0%
9	Materials	144,000	151,200	163,800	12,600	8.3%
10	Labour	240,000	252,000	270,000	18,000	7.1%
11	Overheads	90,000	90,000	92,000	2,000	2.2%
12	**Profit**	**126,000**	**136,800**	**116,800**	**20,000**	**14.6%**
13						

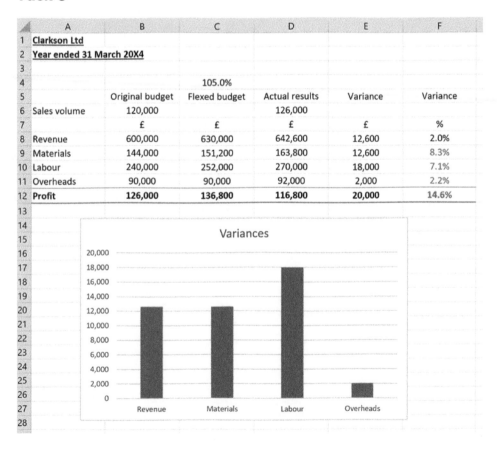

BPP
LEARNING
MEDIA

BPP
LEARNING
MEDIA

TP02-6122-010